Praise for Boxtree's Mo[tley Fool] ... ordinary readers:

The Motley Fool UK In[vestment Guide] number one bestseller:

'(The book) is geared entirely to the UK market and it is difficult to see how anyone could fail to benefit.'
Mail on Sunday

'This book has completely changed the way I look at the world of personal finance… I can't recommend this book enough: funny and informative.' P. Coleman

The Motley Fool UK Investment Workbook

'The most useful investment book of 1999' *Mail on Sunday*

'If you've ever wondered if you needed a pension, whether shares are as risky as they sound or if you simply can't figure out where all your pay cheque went this month, this is an ideal introduction to making your money work for you.' Tim Jordan

The Fool's Guide to Investment Clubs

'A good, easy to understand introduction to investment clubs.' Darren Welch

The Motley Fool UK Web site was the winner of the 1999 *New Media Age* Award for Best Personal Finance Web site and the 1999 *Creative Freedom* Best Electronic Media site.

The following Motley Fool books are also published by
Boxtree:

The Old Fool's Retirement Guide

The Old Fool's Retirement Guide

Rob Davies with David Berger

BⓈXTREE

First published 2001 by Boxtree
an imprint of Macmillan Publishers Ltd
25 Eccleston Place, London, SW1W 9NF
Basingstoke and Oxford

www.macmillan.com

Associated companies throughout the world

ISBN 0 7522 7238 1

A CIP catalogue record for this book is available from
the British Library.

Typeset by Anita Ruddell
Printed and bound in Great Britain by Mackays of Chatham plc, Kent

Acknowledgements

Many people have contributed to this book, some knowingly some unknowingly. My former pension salesman would be among the latter. Many others have contributed to my financial education, what little there is of it, and I would like to thank all of them for their input. In particular I must mention Michael Long who opened the door to the stock market for me. He gave me a great opportunity and taught me so much.

Many years later I am still learning, and Stephen Bland (aka TMF Pyad) has taught me much in the time since I joined the Fool and I am grateful that he has been so free with his thoughts. Though I do wish he would tell us what he really means and not pussy foot around with fancy language. Talking of the Fool of course brings me to the the co-founders David Berger and Bruce Jackson who took a big risk in employing such a Wise person as myself in 1999, when I realised I couldn't cope with the fundamental hypocrisy of the City any longer. I thank them for that opportunity.

My co-writers at the Fool must also be thanked for putting up with occasional bursts of over-exuberance when I discover a new share. My heartfelt thanks go to Chris Spink, Stuart Watson, Maynard Paton and David Kuo. Special thanks go to our editor Martin Wake for rearranging my stuff to make it intelligible. James Carlisle gets an extra-special mention for taking his personal finance knowledge and expertise to spend a good while tweaking the manuscript of this book.

My parents deserve my thanks for all the support they have given me over the years, but it is my immediate family of Chrissie, and my children Georgina and William, who have been most supportive of this reluctant author.

Rob Davies
March 2001

Contents

Foreword

The title of this book wasn't thought up by anyone in particular, but rather popped out of the ether fully formed. There wasn't anything else it could really have been called. Once you've got the words 'Fool', 'Retirement' and 'Guide' gathered together, then 'Old' comes tagging along shortly after and inserts itself firmly before 'Fool'. Luckily, we did have an 'Old Fool' of our own, Rob Davies, whose experience, and not just his age, made him ideally suited to the task of mapping out a path to retirement. In an office composed mainly of people in their twenties and thirties, Rob is distinguished by his hoary memories of the great bear market and worldwide recession of 1973/1974, although from what we can gather he was in Antarctica at the time doing something odd with penguins for the British Antarctic Survey. No matter, *for Rob was there*, in spirit anyway, and since then has built up a phenomenal knowledge and understanding of the financial markets through his work as a City analyst and now at the Fool.

Rob joined us in April 1999 at around the time the UK Motley Fool was starting to coalesce out of cyberspace (mine and co-founder, Bruce Jackson's, home computers) and into an office. Since then the Fool UK has grown to serve hundreds of thousands of individual visitors each month, with many millions of page views on its website and book sales now in the hundreds of thousands. We've been part of the wave that has opened up finance in the past several years in the UK, and I hope and believe that we have contributed both to the direction and the height of that wave. The Motley Fool – in all its manifestations – exists to help you make better financial decisions and that's what this book is all about.

Tell us what you thought of it at **OldFool@fool.co.uk** or else write to

> Old Fool's Retirement Guide
> The Motley Fool UK
> The Media Centre
> 3–8 Carburton Street
> London
> W1W 5AJ

And if you're passing, feel free to pop in and say hello. We're about a hundred yards from Great Portland Street underground station.

> David Berger
> March 2001

* All figures stated in this book are as of end of February 2001.

Chapter 1
The Problem

All progress is based upon a universal innate desire on the part of every organism to live beyond its income.
Samuel Butler

Well, actually there isn't just one problem, there are quite a few. Somehow, there always are. The biggest problem is that as a nation we simply don't save enough readies to ensure a comfortable retirement. Here come some pretty frightening statistics about the state of savings in our country, so hang on to your hats.

According to data from the Office of National Statistics, the country as a whole has precious little in the way of savings. On a national basis, 30 per cent of households have no savings at all and 17 per cent of couples, where one is above pensionable age, are in a similar position.

It's much worse than this, though.

What is even more worrying is the disclosure that while nearly half the country does have savings, they amount to less than £10,000. That really isn't going to go very far. Of course this data excludes illiquid assets (that means assets you can't easily turn into cash) like houses and pensions, so the total wealth is much higher. Nevertheless, value tied up in a house is not much use if you need to buy a pint of milk in the morning.

Of course, simple logic tells us that we would not

expect the average family to have a lot of savings. In most cases all available income goes on the necessities of life like the mortgage, food and the never-ending cash requirements of children. (Tell me about it!) These heavy cash requirements, combined with historical attitudes towards savings (it's something for tomorrow), mean that it has only been towards the end of most people's lives that they have started to accumulate some cash, so it is slightly more encouraging to read that 30 per cent of couples where one or both are above pensionable age have savings of £20,000 or more. Even so, as we shall see later, that still won't go very far.

Here is another number to drive the point home. Only 8 per cent of families consisting of two adults below retirement age and with one or more children have savings of £20,000 or more. Considering this represents pretty much the typical family, it doesn't sound too encouraging. Although this family probably has several decades of good income from one or more parents ahead of it, there will also be many other demands on their cash. Perhaps the point is made more starkly by reversing it. Put this way, we see that 92 per cent of families with one or more children have savings of less than £20,000. Ninety-two per cent!

And here is the final number to leave you either quaking in your boots or tut-tutting over your morning cup of tea about the financial imprudence of your compatriots. When people tot up their savings (and these ONS statistics are self-reported, which means that savings are what people think they are), for some reason they generally don't think of their pension, so you may be saying to yourself: 'They may not have that much in the way of savings, but I bet many of those people have reasonable pensions.'

You think that? You really do?

No, you've just been set up. The average premium paid into a personal pension in the UK (we go into personal pensions later and whether they're a decent investment or not, but suffice to say here that they are an investment for your retirement) is about £300 *a year*. That is nowhere near enough to buy a decent retirement and if £300 is the average, then that means that many, and probably most, of the contributions are less than that. Anyway, as we'll see later, a big chunk of what gets paid into personal pensions often goes out right away in fees to the adviser who sold it or to the management company that administers it, so it's not as if that £300 is even going straight into your investments. The situation with occupational pensions is even worse. Today, it is estimated that only 1 per cent of people will retire with a full occupational pension.

So what does all this mean for you? Well, there's one simple lesson to draw from all this, so turn over the page for the Most Important Foolish Rule of Retirement Investing (and try saying that rapidly ten times after six pink gins):

SAVE MORE!

At the Motley Fool, we find there's nothing like a little British understatement to really drive a point home.

The next major problem is that you're living too long. Well, OK, *you're* not, it's more like we all are. Life expectancy is steadily rising and has been for a long while (a woman's life expectancy was 54 years at birth in 1911, 79.7 years now and is expected to get to 82.7 years in 2021), which means that the number of retired people is rising. Unfortunately, the number of workers is rising more slowly.

Now, living to a ripe old age is generally regarded as a good thing, but it represents a real headache for the government which has to fund the state pension out of the National Insurance contributions of people who are working, in other words out of taxation. It's all down to the famous baby boom of the post-war years, which is still working its way through the demographics of the UK like – if you'll forgive a stomach-squelching analogy – a pig lunch progressing through a python. So far the bulge has reached its mid-40s and mostly it is still in paid employment. But in ten years' time it will have started to reach retirement age and will start to pass out of the workforce. Then the dynamics of the tax system, and the load on government services, will become more unequal. A shrinking workforce will have to support, through the tax system, a generation of pensioners who will still need services like roads, policing and, especially, the health service. What's more, they'll need these services for longer.

And now it's time for a little bit of history.

A little bit of history

In the so-called 'good old days', or at least back when Britain thought it could afford a bountiful welfare state, the state pension grew each year in line with average earnings. Over the years, we have grown wealthier as a nation, which is demonstrated by the fact that average earnings have historically grown by roughly 2 per cent more than the rate of inflation each year. This doesn't sound like much, but year on year the difference gets huger and huger, as we'll see in chapter 3 when we talk about the miracle of compound interest. Mrs Thatcher and her government in 1981 realised that they, and their successors, were facing a blank cheque of enormous proportions if they continued to allow pensions to grow at 2 per cent above the rate of inflation. They therefore shifted the linkage from average earnings down to the rate of inflation. Only 2 per cent? What's 2 per cent between friends?

Well, it is estimated that the single person's pension today would be over £100, as compared to the current £67.50, if that earnings link had been maintained. In other words, the spending power of the state pensioner has declined significantly relative to the average wage. To put it bluntly: pensioners have become a lot poorer in relation to those who are still working.

Today's Labour government has declined to restore the earnings link, realising how much it would cost in ten or twenty years, despite the impassioned pleas of Barbara Castle and Jack Jones and despite being defeated on the motion by the delegates at the 2000 Labour Party conference. (To give them some credit, though, they have instead put in place a couple of fairly hefty pension increases over the next several years.) Meanwhile, Mrs

Thatcher criticized the Labour government at the 2000 Conservative Party conference for not restoring the earnings link to pensions – yet it was she who took it away in the first place.

Go figure!

Anyway, the long and short of it is that the Nanny State, 'cradle to grave' and all that, was a marvellous, noble concept. Unfortunately, the numbers don't work. An infinite demand from people to be looked after cannot be met by a finite amount of money raised from voters who would prefer to spend it on themselves. At best the state old age pension is only ever going to provide the most basic amount of support. Most of us will want significantly more than that to be comfortable.

What would be most convenient, of course, would be for us all to die earlier and have a few more kids. It would solve a lot of problems. Since that isn't going to happen, you had better start making your own arrangements for old age. Picking up this book is a good start. Flicking over the page and moving on to the next chapter, 'How Much Do You Need?', is an excellent next step.

Chapter 2

How Much Do You Need?

A large income is the best recipe for happiness I ever heard of.
It certainly may secure all the myrtle and turkey part of it.
Jane Austen, *Mansfield Park*

By now you should be convinced that there'll be little help from the state for your retirement, something you probably weren't too surprised to hear. That means we're all faced, as a matter of urgency, with building a large enough pot of money to fund our retirement life. This chapter aims to look at the size of the challenge facing us. Before we start, though, don't panic! Some of the numbers we are going to see here look large, but they are achievable.

Telling someone how much they need to live on is as silly as suggesting they buy certain clothes: much will depend on preference, lifestyle, health, dependants and geography, to name just a few factors. Nevertheless, we can use some numbers from the family expenditure survey of the Office of National Statistics to put us in the general region, or at least give us something to work from. In 1997 the average family spent £331 a week, but that figure covers a range from £171 for the bottom fifth to £556 for the top fifth of the population. Clearly the composition of the weekly expenditure between the two ends of the spectrum will be sharply different. For example, those in the top fifth spend 20 per cent of their outgoings on leisure goods and services, while those in the bottom fifth spend only 13 per cent on that category.

These differences are also seen between different age groups; the charity Age Concern reckons that in households where the head is over 65, 40 per cent of the expenditure goes on housing, fuel and food. Pensioners living alone spend nearly 50 per cent on these essential items. The average for the country as a whole is 36 per cent.

This increased proportion of spending on essentials reflects the fact that the average person retiring today is not going to be among the most well-off in society. In fact they are far more likely to be among the less well-off. Set against that is the fact that, by and large, they will not have any dependants and their outgoings will be less. If the kids haven't flown the coop by then, they at least *ought* to be contributing to the household income. (Send them round to us if they're not and we'll give them an earful on your behalf.)

As that data from the ONS is a little bit old, and to make things easy, how about we use a figure of £200 a week as the rough average minimum outgoings needed to run a house and generally keep ticking along, assuming the mortgage is paid off? In round terms that equates to just over £10,000 a year needed to run the average home reasonably comfortably.

That's what the *average* home needs to run comfortably, but we want to know how much it is going to cost to run *our* home comfortably. If you want to retire early, you may be prepared for a significant 'downshift' in your lifestyle. We talk about this later in the book. But most of us probably want to maintain our standard of living in retirement, so let's look at how to go about it. Firstly, what's your current standard of living? If you're relatively young, that will change over time, hopefully for the better (but possibly for the worse). The yardstick we'll need to work from is the standard of living that you expect prior to retirement. That means looking realistically at what you expect to be earning just before you collect your gold watch.

But maintaining your standard of living in retirement doesn't necessarily mean having precisely the same income. It means having the same *disposable* income. So, assuming that you've paid off your mortgage and your kids (if any) have left home, you'll need a lot less income to keep yourself comfortable than you did at some stages of your working life. It might also be that you plan to move to somewhere where things are a bit cheaper. Not necessarily the south of Spain, but just moving from, say, London to the south coast or somewhere nice in the country might make quite a difference.

Bear in mind that, if you've paid off your mortgage, moving into a cheaper house may not actually cut your outgoings as much as you think. Heating bills, dilapidation costs and council tax may be a little less, but it may not make all that much difference to your monthly outlay. What exchanging your house for a smaller version does do for you, however, is free up more money to invest to provide an income.

It's also true that you might have additional expenses in retirement. You will have more time on your hands to fill with your hobbies. It's a wonderful thought, but it might cost a bit, particularly if that hobby is sailing on hyper-expensive Russian icebreaker cruises to the North Pole or flying World War II fighters.

It's all a question of formulating a realistic picture in your mind's eye of where exactly you're likely to be when retirement comes around. You need to sit down with a pencil and a piece of paper, or a computer with a spreadsheet program open, and list your expenses today versus what you think they may be when you retire. And, in the best Delia Smith tradition, here's one we prepared earlier. Actually, we didn't prepare it, a poster on our online discussion boards by the online name of SarcoramphusPapa prepared it. He has kindly allowed us to publish it here and this is what he estimated his expenses to be, before and after retirement:

Current essentials		*Retirement essentials*	
Council Tax	£60	Council Tax	£60
Water	£35	Water	£35
Electric/Gas	£20	Electric/Gas	£20
Mortgage	£800	Mortgage	£00
Endowment	£60	Endowment	£00
Life Assurance	£45	Life Assurance	£45
Home Insurance	£25	Home Insurance	£25
Health Plan	£60	Health Plan	£60
Food/Groceries	£200	Food/Groceries	£200
Commuting	£150	Commuting	£00
Monthly (min)	**£1,455**	**Monthly (min)**	**£445**

Current conveniences		Retirement conveniences	
Car (run, tax, ins)	£100	Car (run, tax, ins)	£130
TV	£10	TV	£10
Misc	£200	Misc	£300
Subtotal	£310	Subtotal	£440
Monthly (min)	£1,455	Monthly (min)	£445
Monthly (ave)	**£1,765**	**Monthly (ave)**	**£885**

Current luxuries		Retirement luxuries	
Holidays	£200	Holidays	£400
Horse	£200	Horse	£200
Dog	£40	Dogs	£80
2nd Car	£60	2nd Car	£50
Gym	£20	Gym	£20
Misc	£100	Misc	£150
Subtotal	£620	Subtotal	£900
Monthly (ave)	£1,765	Monthly (ave)	£885
Monthly (Lux)	**£2,385**	**Monthly (Lux)**	**£1,785**

SarcoramphusPapa is going to need an annual, after-tax retirement income of just over £21,000. To help you with your own figures, here is the same table, with some extra spaces so you can add some of your own items. Pencils out!

Current essentials		*Retirement essentials*	
Council Tax	£	Council Tax	£
Water	£	Water	£
Electric/Gas	£	Electric/Gas	£
Mortgage	£	Mortgage	£
Endowment	£	Endowment	£
Life Assurance	£	Life Assurance	£
Home Insurance	£	Home Insurance	£
Health Plan	£	Health Plan	£
Food/Groceries	£	Food/Groceries	£
Commuting	£	Commuting	£
....	£	....	£
....	£	....	£
....	£	....	£
....	£	....	£
....	£	....	£
....	£	....	£
Monthly (min)	£	**Monthly (min)**	£

Current conveniences		*Retirement conveniences*	
Car (run, tax, ins)	£	Car (run, tax, ins)	£
TV	£	TV	£
....	£	....	£
....	£	....	£
....	£	....	£
....	£	....	£
....	£	....	£
Misc	£	Misc	£
Subtotal	£	Subtotal	£

Monthly (min)	£	Monthly (min)	£

Monthly (ave)	£	**Monthly (ave)**	£

Current luxuries		*Retirement luxuries*	
Holidays	£	Holidays	£
Horse	£	Horse	£
Dog	£	Dog	£
2nd Car	£	2nd Car	£
Gym	£	Gym	£
....	£	....	£
....	£	....	£
....	£	....	£
....	£	....	£
....	£	....	£
Misc	£	Misc	£

Subtotal	£	Subtotal	£
Monthly (ave)	£	Monthly (ave)	£

Monthly (lux)	£	**Monthly (lux)**	£

Everyone's figures will be different, but for the purposes of this book we are going to need a sum to aim for. Although £10,000 a year in today's values may be just about sufficient for most people to live on, this means they won't be going on any fancy foreign holidays and will not be leading a luxurious lifestyle in any way. Since we are Fools, and we have higher targets than the bare minimum, let's shoot for a little more, for £15,000. That will be achievable by many people with a bit of planning, and if you add on the current state pension (roughly

£5,000 per year) you probably won't be doing too badly; although, as we've seen, in relative terms that state pension is going to mean less and less as time goes on.

So, we're going to use £15,000 throughout this book, for the purposes of simplicity and because we think it's a reasonable average target for many people. It may not be the right amount for you: as you filled out the table above you may have come to the conclusion that you'd be able to scrape by on £7,000 a year on your croft in the Outer Hebrides, or that you may need £70,000 a year to keep your mansion running in the wilds of Surrey. (If it's the latter, I'm always open to invitations for a gin and tonic. If it's the former, I'll pass on the opportunity to herd sheep on the side of a 3,000-foot mountain in a driving gale.) Whatever your target, though, the basic points about achieving it are the same. What follows in the rest of the chapter is a look at just a few of the further issues that will influence how much you're going to need to salt away.

But what about inflation?

Everything that we've considered so far is in terms of today's money but, as we all know, a pound in twenty years' time is likely to buy us quite a lot less than it can buy us now. So, how do we factor inflation into our calculations? Although it might at first seem like we're burying our heads in the sand, the Foolish solution to this is simply to ignore it.

We can do this because we can then ignore inflation with our investments as well. For instance, if we expect inflation to be 3 per cent per year and we plan to retire in twenty years' time, then we'd need about 80 per cent more money to fund our retirement than we'd need if we were to retire on that income today. BUT, we'd expect our investments to have grown at that extra 3 per cent per year as well, so our retirement pot would also have grown by 80 per cent. That means that since we'd have to factor inflation into both sides of the equation, and we have no firm idea what it will be, the best thing to do is to leave it out altogether and plan for our retirement with an investment return that does not include inflation. Since we're removing it from both sides, we end up back where we started. Got that? If you haven't, read it again because it's an important point.

It goes further than this, though. When we deal with inflation in this way, common sense tells us we should be able to get to whatever income we need to buy the things that we buy now (and expect to need in retirement, too). However, if we'd thought that in the 1960s, then we'd now be consigned to a retirement driving around in a Ford Prefect, with no microwave oven, no computer and no video recorder. In fact, we wouldn't even have allowed for a telly!

Generally, if we want to maintain our standard of living into retirement, what we actually want is to maintain our relative position in the economy as a whole. This means that we need our retirement income, and our investments, to keep up not just with inflation, but with increases in the average wages that people earn.

As with inflation, we can account for 'growth in average earnings' in our expected investment returns. Over the years, it has amounted to about 2 per cent per year above inflation.

So, remember that we're ignoring inflation and are going to account for growth in average earnings from whatever investment return we think we may get. We'll come back to this in a short while.

Long-term investment returns

Having determined how much we need to live on, the next thing we need to determine is the size of the pot that will generate the income we need. This is going to depend crucially on two things: our desired level of income (remember we're using £15,000 at today's values as our jumping-off point) and the return we can expect to get on our pot of savings. The issue of long-term investment returns is the subject of much discussion, within the Fool, within society, within the government, everywhere in fact. It is such a very hot topic because the financial futures of so many individuals in the country depend on it and, at the time of writing, it is particularly in the news as a result of what much of the press is calling the endowments mis-selling scandal. This revolves around the fact that the returns on endowments are now expected to be nowhere near as high as the (commission-based) salesmen claimed they would be when they were sold. The Financial Services Authority, the government body charged with overseeing the financial services industry, has therefore revised its projected investment returns from endowments down to 6 per cent per year. That means that if they only hit that projected growth rate, a lot of endowments will not pay off the mortgage they are supposed to be covering.

What kind of long-term returns should we be aiming for, then? Unfortunately, there's no simple answer. We have to delve a little deeper and look at the different classes of investments.

Ready? Let's start with our old friend, the High Street bank.

Banks

Really, banks are great places. You can cash cheques there, buy foreign currency to go on holiday, and do all sorts of good, worthy and useful things in them. But overly adventurous they are not. They like borrowing money from you at 5 per cent and lending it to your brother at 12 per cent until he pays off his overdraft. Since that is basically never, the bank is on to a winner. As long as most people keep paying the interest on their loans then it makes a good living out of lending money to business and consumers.

Lending money to the bank (i.e. opening a deposit account) is, by and large, risk free. The chances are that when you come back in 45 years to pick up that money, the bank will still be there – different name perhaps, but it will still be there and will be delighted to give you all your money back plus the interest you are due. After all, they've been lending out your money to other people at rates considerably higher than they were paying you. Don't worry, though: if something nasty happens to those people borrowing your money – for example, they go bust and can't pay the money back – it is the bank that suffers, not you. Your money is lent to the bank (not directly to your brother, so you can wipe the sweat from your brow) and it is up to the bank to make sure you get every penny back, with interest. The reason they are able to charge higher interest to borrowers than they pay to savers like you is that they are taking this risk on their own shoulders. If you like, they're getting paid to take risk, an important idea that we'll return to shortly.

For now, though, just remember that long term, *really* long term, a bank has historically paid you, on average, around a 5 per cent return (aka 'interest') on your investment each year. However, that's before we take off inflation and average earnings growth. After deducting inflation, banks have historically paid only 1.6 per cent and, after taking away our 2 per cent for average earnings growth, we have a figure which is, err, less than zero.

Banks, then, are very handy for keeping a specific sum of money safe for a short period of time but, for long-term retirement planning, they've been pretty useless in the past and there isn't much reason to see this changing.

Who else can we lend money to, other than a bank?

Why, the government of course! A bank can go bust and that means it won't be able to pay your money back. It's exceedingly unlikely for this to happen to a major bank in Britain – although it does happen in many other countries. Nevertheless, the government is even less likely to go bust than, say, Lloyds TSB (since, apart from anything else, it prints the actual money!). Lending money to the government involves buying 'gilts' and long term, *really* long term, gilts have returned, on average, just a tad more than cash in a deposit account. About 6 per cent, in fact. After we take the inflation axe to it, though, this falls to just over 2 per cent per year and, after our allowance for growth in average earnings, we end up fractionally above zero.

At the moment, long-term gilts are offering returns

of around 4.5 per cent before inflation, which is actually less than cash. The flip side is that this rate of return is guaranteed for many years, whereas the bank can change its rates at a moment's notice and indeed is likely to do so. Long-term gilts return a bit less than cash because the balance of opinion among investors is that interest rates over the next decade or two are most likely headed downwards. As a result, people are prepared to accept a slightly lower, but guaranteed, rate.

What else can I do apart from lending money?

Lending money to a bank or the government brings you a steady, reliable return on your investment, but not a huge one. The way to earn more money over the long term, much more, is to become an *owner of equity capital*, rather than a *supplier of debt capital*. Sounds impressive, doesn't it? 'Darling, enough of debt financing! Enough! I've decided we shall henceforth become owners of equity capital.' Try it out on your spouse or partner tonight. Chances are you'll be met with a blank stare, but all it means is you've decided to invest in shares.

If you have a bank deposit account or you buy gilts, you are lending money (*capital*) to an organization that is in*debted* to you. On the other hand, if you buy shares in a company you are becoming a part-owner of something tangible, i.e. you are buying *equity* in a company. It's a completely different kettle of fish. As the owner of a company, you take much, much more risk than you do by lending money to a bank or the government. Much more. On the other hand, you have much, much more to gain. Much more.

Historically, UK shares (or *equities* – and now you understand why they're called that) have returned around 12 per cent annually. Taking off inflation, this return comes down to about 8 per cent per year and knocking off average earnings growth of 2 per cent leaves us with a historic return of 6 per cent. As we'll see in the next chapter, the difference between this return and those of gilts or banks means a dramatic difference in long-term growth.

You may by now be asking what all this is based on. Well, heaps of studies have shown that over the long term, equities have outperformed all other classes of investments by a country mile. The figure we tend to use at the Motley Fool is the 12 per cent nominal growth in equities since 1918, calculated by the boffins at Credit Suisse First Boston and published every year in their Equity-Gilt Study.

Nominal returns (i.e. including inflation) from 1918 to 1999

    Equities 12.3%
    Gilts   6.2%
    Cash   5.5%
Source: Credit Suisse First Boston Equity-Gilt Study for 1999

Going back even further, to 1869, the data is just as conclusive.

Nominal returns from 1869 to 1999

    Equities 9.8%
    Gilts   4.7%
    Cash   4.7%
Source: Credit Suisse First Boston Equity-Gilt Study for 1999

It's tempting to project these numbers forward in a straight line and say the next fifty or hundred years will be more or less like the last. The last hundred years have seen more technological and political change than the last 1,500, including the dismantling of the British Empire, the rise and fall of communism, as well as the invention of a variety of machines from cars, aeroplanes and nuclear power to the Internet, while not forgetting the Frisbee. You could argue that it is this exceptional pace of change and tremendous growth that has fuelled the rise in share prices around the world, and that is undoubtedly true. After all, it is companies that create the wealth that drives social and political change. They do this by taking a business idea, investing capital in it, perhaps your capital, and developing it into a going concern that adds real value. The invested money is worth more because it has made a return, and generated cash or a greater value for the assets employed. Buying shares is therefore not like buying stamps or gold, which have value because of their rarity. Companies can easily create more shares (although this dilutes the value of your holding), so shares are not in finite supply like rare stamps or works of art. A share entitles you to part-ownership of a business, and that business hopefully grows over time and generates cash that it can pass on to its shareholders.

But is this exceptional period of wealth creation about to come to an end? No one can say for sure, of course, and as was mentioned earlier, it is a subject of intense debate, on the Motley Fool's online discussion boards as much as anywhere else. Looked at from here, though, there seems to be no slowdown in the rate of change and development, which, if anything, has speeded up; and it seems more reasonable to base assumptions for the coming fifty years on the experience of the last hundred or so, rather than going back to, say, 1066, when the closest most people got to share ownership was once a week with the village plough.

Whatever the exact level of the returns that we get from shares in the future, we think it's a pretty safe bet that, over the very long term (by which we mean 20 or 30 years or more), shares will, on average, keep doing better than cash and gilts. This is because of where the interest on cash and gilts actually comes from. It doesn't just materialize out of thin air; it has to be earned. The government earns the bulk of its money from tax – tax on the profits made by companies, tax on the wages paid by companies and tax on the things that we buy from companies. Banks make most of their money by lending to companies that pay the interest out of their profits. Companies are the bottom line in the economy and, one way or another, policy must be set so that they keep ticking along.

The risks of shares

Despite all this, there is no doubt that investing in shares involves risks. Each individual company has a highly uncertain value and is very risky (at least in comparison to cash and gilts). There are two ways of getting around this, which can be called 'stock diversification' and 'time diversification'.

Stock diversification is quite simple. It just means buying lots of different companies. Basically, you hedge your bets. At the extreme end of things, you could own a slice of every company on the stock market – in direct proportion to the size of that company. In a sense, you're buying a slice of what many people call 'UK plc'. You can do this by buying something called an 'index tracker' (which we'll talk about more later) and it certainly goes a long way to reducing the risk of shares. However, studies have shown that you only actually need to split up your money (fairly evenly) between 12 to 15 different companies (in a range of different industries) to have a pretty similar effect.

Even if we're spread across many companies, or the entire stock market through an index tracker, the returns of the stock market *average* from year to year can vary a great deal too. The solution to this is *time* diversification. Although the performance of the UK economy (and investors' perception of it) can vary a lot from year to year, it doesn't vary nearly so much over longer periods. Investing over a lot of years has a similar risk-spreading effect to investing in a lot of different companies.

So, by buying a basket of different shares and investing for the long term, you can reduce the risk of shares enormously. In fact, as we'll see in a moment, over periods as long as 20 or 30 years, shares turn out to be less risky, in real terms, than cash and gilts. We can see how time diversification works by looking at some more data from the CSFB Equity-Gilt Study. What we're looking at are the 'real' returns (that is, returns once inflation has been taken off) on the different classes of asset for various time periods since 1918. Hold on to your hats, off we go.

One-year real returns since 1918

	Average annual return (%)	Highest annual return (%)	Lowest annual return (%)
Equities	8.2	99.7	-58.1
Gilts	2.3	57.8	-28.9
Cash	1.6	41.7	-11.3

Equities outperformed gilts in 66.7% of years.
Equities outperformed cash in 63.0% of years.

Not surprisingly, we see that equities have the best average annual returns of 8.2 per cent: in other words by investing in equities you're getting paid to take risk. By comparison, the returns of gilts (2.3 per cent) and cash (1.6 per cent) look decidedly sick. However, we also see that equities are by far the most risky asset over one-year periods. Their returns varied between 99.7 per cent (in 1975) and minus 58.1 per cent (in 1974). (1974 and 1975, the height of the oil crisis and the 'three-day week', was a pretty rocky time for shares!).

What this tells us is that if you know you're going to need a specific sum of money in a year's time, then you shouldn't put it anywhere near the stock market. It should stay in cash. Even so, cash isn't as safe, in post-inflation terms, as you probably thought. Its real returns varied between plus 41.7 per cent (the deflationary year of 1921, when prices of goods dropped through the floor) and minus 11.3 per cent (the inflationary year of 1975, when prices of goods shot through the roof). Now let's have a look at five-year periods.

Rolling five-year real returns since 1918

	Average annual return (%)	Highest annual return (%)	Lowest annual return (%)
Equities	8.2	32.1	-18.8
Gilts	2.3	19.4	-10.8
Cash	1.6	12.5	-4.9

Equities outperformed gilts in 79.7% of five-year periods.
Equities outperformed cash in 75.9% of five-year periods.

Well that's looking a lot better for shares already. What we're looking at are 'rolling five-year periods'. So, the first is 1918–1923, the second is 1919–1924, then 1920–1925... you get the picture. We still have the same average annual returns (it has to work out like that – that's maths for you) but, already, the range of returns for equities has fallen from a massive 158 percentage points for the yearly returns to 51 percentage points for these five-year periods. Still quite high, though. How about ten years?

Rolling ten-year real returns since 1918

	Average annual return (%)	Highest annual return (%)	Lowest annual return (%)
Equities	8.2	18.5	-6.0
Gilts	2.3	13.5	-6.9
Cash	1.6	9.8	-3.3

Equities outperformed gilts in 93.1% of ten-year periods. Equities outperformed cash in 97.2% of ten-year periods.

Now the writing is quietly going up on the wall for cash and gilts. Ten years is about as long as they can make sense as investments. If you don't believe us, look again at the table. In particular, the bit underneath. Equities did better than cash in 97 per cent of ten-year periods and they beat gilts in 93 per cent of them. What's more, even in the worst ten-year period for equities (1964–1974), they only lost 6 per cent. Even cash lost 3.3 per cent in its worst period (1969–1979). So, on this evidence, you're not taking much of a risk by going for equities and you've generally been repaid handsomely for doing so. Now we'll move on to 20 years.

Rolling 20-year real returns since 1918

	Average annual return (%)	Highest annual return (%)	Lowest annual return (%)
Equities	8.2	13.3	0.3
Gilts	2.3	8.4	-4.5
Cash	1.6	4.7	-2.6

Equities outperformed gilts in 100% of 20-year periods. Equities outperformed cash in 98.4% of 20-year periods.

Stop the game! That's it, gilts and cash have finally thrown in the towel. Looking at these numbers there is very little to say for cash and gilts as investments over a 20-year period.

In real terms, equities have beaten gilts in every single 20-year period since 1918 and they have beaten cash in all but one of them. Surprise, surprise, it's 1954–1974 (1974 has a lot to answer for!). Even in that period, equities lost to cash by just 0.3 per cent per year (and if you'd held on to the shares for one more year, everything would have been rosy since equities had their best year ever, a real gain of 99.7 per cent, in 1975). On top of that, the worst 20-year periods for gilts and cash provided annual returns of minus 4.5 per cent and minus 2.6 per cent. At least the worst 20-year period for shares showed a positive return (0.3 per cent), even if it didn't amount to very much. OK, finally, let's have a look at 30-year periods. Just for fun, you understand.

Rolling 30-year real returns since 1918

	Average annual return (%)	Highest annual return (%)	Lowest annual return (%)
Equities	8.2	9.4	2.0
Gilts	2.3	5.6	-4.3
Cash	1.6	2.4	-1.3

Equities outperformed gilts in 100% of 30-year periods.
Equities outperformed cash in 100% of 30-year periods.

There isn't really much to say about this. Shhh… we don't want to rub their faces in it. Oh go on then, in its *best* 30-year period, cash managed a measly real return of 2.4 per cent per year. By contrast, equities returned 2.0 per cent in their *worst* 30-year period. Nuff said.

Pulling it all together

So what are we to make of all this? Well, first of all, we can see that cash in a bank account is probably the best place to store money for short periods of time. However, as our investing period gets longer, shares make more and more sense. Since retirement planning, and even retirement itself (we hope), involves periods of upwards of 20 years, then shares look very much like the best bet. So long as, of course, we spread our risk properly over a number of different companies.

What actual level of return to expect from the different assets, however, is more difficult. The trouble is that you have to come up with a figure of some sort, otherwise you can't make any plans. So, what figure to go for? Many people will tell you that the market is 'looking a bit high at the moment' and many will tell you that 'it's looking pretty cheap'. The fact is that there will always be competing opinions, since that is what makes a market.

So what are we going to settle on as our planning figure for projected investment return? Let's start with the 8 per cent real return that shares have given since 1918, and subtract yearly investment charges of 0.5 per cent to give 7.5 per cent. It's likely that shares will perform at this level in the future. There's no very good reason to think otherwise. But let's be really, really conservative and account for average earnings growth of 2 per cent; subtracting it from this figure, we can bank on a return of 5.5 per cent to use for our retirement projections. What this means is that we'll be pleasantly surprised when our investment returns 7.5 per cent (something we secretly hope and half expect to happen). If that does occur, our investment will have grown not only in line with inflation, which is essential, but average earnings too, which is very nice. It's better to plan for 5.5 per cent and expect to be pleasantly surprised than to plan for 7.5 per cent and hope not to be disappointed. It's a slightly awkward number, but it's our best guess and, as we'll see in a moment, it does have the advantage of throwing up pretty-looking numbers when you divide things by it.

Of course, although it's very unlikely, we might end up doing worse. We could argue for eons about what the future returns of the stock market will be, and if you come along to our website you'll find people discussing this very issue on our discussion boards. Here's the thing, though: we have to plant a flag in the ground and come up with a number of some sort; and as long as we review our retirement plan regularly, we should be able to compensate for poor stock market performance by increasing our saving along the way. 5.5 per cent it is.

So how much do *you need?*

Well, after all that talk of investment returns, it seems a while ago since we were asking this question. Now, though, we're in a better position to answer it. Assuming that we are making an investment return of 5.5 per cent (remember, in *real* terms: that is, taking inflation into account. Hopefully, too, this number is sufficiently conservative for us to outperform it by a couple of per cent, thus accounting for growth in average earnings and keeping us as 'relatively' wealthy as the rest of society), then we can take 5.5 per cent out of our pot of money each year and the pot will still maintain its real value. What we therefore need to focus on is a pot of money, 5.5 per cent of which comes to £15,000. This gives us the following sum:

Pot x 5.5% = £15,000

We can rearrange this by dividing both sides by 5.5% to give

Pot = £15,000 / 5.5%

Remembering that 5.5% is 0.055, we have

Pot = £15,000 / 0.055 = £272,727

Let's call it a round(ish) £275,000 for simplicity.

Wow. Let's let that sink in for a moment. Roll it around our tongues for a while. Two hundred and seventy-five grand. A bit over a quarter of a million, minimum. That's an awful lot of spondoolicks.

Wow! 275K. Wow!

You may need less than this level of income, you may need more, depending on your lifestyle and expectations, but you now have a useful ready reckoner for calculating how big your retirement fund will have to be, based on how much income you'll need.

For instance, if you're going for the back-to-nature, crofting lifestyle on the draughty island of Harris, you'll need a pot of money 5.5 per cent of which comes to £7,000. So…

Pot x 0.055 = £7,000

Tum de tum…

Pot = £7,000 / 0.055 = £127,272

And clinking the cocktail glasses in Surrey?

Pot x 0.055 = £70,000

So (jumping ahead a step)…

Pot = £1,272,728

All this is in today's money and it assumes that we've got our whole pot invested in shares (in reality we might keep a small pile of cash in the bank for unforeseen additional spending needs). We've also assumed that we pay no tax which, to say the least, is a tad optimistic. In the real world, you'll have to pay more or less tax depending on the level of your retirement income and how you've gone about your investing (which is something we'll come on to in later chapters). The way to factor this in is to adjust the rate of return you use. So, if we expect to be paying tax at 20 per cent on our retirement income, then we'd need to take a fifth (that is, 20 per cent) away from our expected return of 5.5 per cent. That would leave us getting only 4.4 per cent. For our target income of £15,000, that means we would need £340,909 (although, because of personal allowances and the 10 per cent tax band, an income of £15,000 is currently taxed at a fair bit less than 20 per cent overall).

Anyway, we've seen that for an income of around £15,000 per year we need to cobble together about £275,000, or in fact a little more when we take into account our cash buffer and a little tax, so let's call it £300,000 to make all the sums simpler. That's a lot of money, but it is achievable. Hopefully this book can show you how. The very next chapter will help set you on your way.

Chapter 3
How do you get that much?

There are few ways in which a man can be more innocently employed than in getting money.
Samuel Johnson

We now know that you probably need to put away something in the range of £130,000 to £1,300,000 in today's values to fund your retirement, depending on whether you're a Surrey cocktail party-goer or a Hebridean shepherd, and also depending on what projected return rate you choose to use. For the reasons already explained, we're opting for £300,000 as our rule of thumb amount to illustrate the points we want to make in this book. That feels like a lot of money.

And it is.

Nevertheless, it is not totally unobtainable.

Consider this. In an average lifetime, the average worker will earn about a million pounds. 'Impossible!' you cry from the armchair. But wait, oh impetuous faint heart. The average wage is a touch over £22,300 a year, and a normal working life has classically been from age 18 to age 65. Yes, I know it is shorter if you go to college, and especially if you study something complicated like medicine or law, but then again, graduates and especially lawyers and doctors earn more than the average wage so it all comes out in the wash. Now, stop nitpicking and multiply 22,300 by 45 years.

The answer is £1,003,500. Got that? I'll spell it out for you, one million, three thousand and five hundred quid. Who needs the lottery or the pools? We can all be millionaires. Wahey!

You could easily earn over a million pounds during the course of your working life. In fact, you could easily earn very significantly more, because your earnings will rise above the rate of inflation, even if you never secure a higher-paying job. To keep it simple, though, as we explained in the previous chapter, we're going to leave out inflation and growth in average earnings.

A million pounds is a fair amount more than the £300,000 we were just talking about. Even so, though, asking someone on the average wage to save 30 per cent of his or her income before tax is a pretty tall, in fact an unattainable, order.

Luckily, we don't have to do that.

Even better, we can solve two problems at once: a worrying storage problem and the growth problem. Let's ask our average wage earner to make what is admittedly still a big effort on a salary like this, and save just over 10 per cent of his income every year: £2,400. That's a relatively achievable £200 per month and it adds up to £108,000 over the 45 years, an awful lot of pound coins, even if it's still far short of the £300,000 we need. If we take those coins to the bank we won't have a storage and weight problem. Even better, we won't have a security problem. After all, we don't want some thief to come along at midnight and shovel our wealth into his swag bag. I am sure it is perfectly possible to work out how many swag bags he would need to carry off £108,000 worth of one pound coins, but I'm not going to do that. Suffice to say it will take him a long time to carry the money away.

So, the bank can store our money for us. But there is a bonus. Unlike a normal warehouse, the bank pays *you* to let them look after *your* money, as we saw in the last chapter. This quaint notion, called interest, is money for old rope. All you have to do is deposit the money with them and they pay you for the privilege, lending it on to other people for higher rates than they pay you, again as we saw in the last chapter. But this is the best part: after a year, when you have earned interest on your first lot of savings, that interest is added to your savings and you get interest on that too. Not only is this money for old rope, it's got knobs on. So fantastic is this invention that it's even got its own name: *compound interest*.

The thing about compound interest is that it means your savings mount up more and more each year. In mathematics, this is known as exponential growth. We devote a fair amount of space to this on our website, where we call it 'The Miracle of Compound Interest', and in our other books, you'll also find compound interest calculators at various places on the Internet. The tables you will see below show just how powerful it is.

Bank accounts, after we've taken off inflation and accounted for the rise in average earnings, have actually paid *negative* interest over the years (of about minus 0.4 per cent). In fact, when we work it out, saving £200 per month at the historic rates that banks have achieved would leave us with a purchasing power of just £98,804 in today's values, after allowing for 45 years of inflation and rising earnings. That's less than the £108,000 we've put aside. Of course, after the previous chapter, you'll probably know the solution to this. What we need is something that produces a better long-term return. What we need is shares. Using shares we can factor in annual growth of at least 5.5 per cent.

If we save at a rate of £200 per month and get an annual return of 5.5 per cent, then our pot grows like this:

Year	End of year total pot value	Year	End of year total pot value
1	£2,471	2	£5,078
3	£7,828	4	£10,729
5	£13,790	6	£17,020
7	£20,427	8	£24,021
9	£27,813	10	£31,814
11	£36,034	12	£40,487
13	£45,185	14	£50,141
15	£55,370	16	£60,886
17	£66,706	18	£72,846
19	£79,323	20	£86,157
21	£93,366	22	£100,972
23	£108,997	24	£117,462
25	£126,394	26	£135,816
27	£145,757	28	£156,245
29	£167,309	30	£178,982
31	£191,297	32	£204,289
33	£217,996	34	£232,457
35	£247,713	36	£263,808
37	£280,788	38	£298,702
39	£317,602	40	£337,541
41	£358,577	42	£380,769
43	£404,183	44	£428,884
45	£454,943		

After 45 years, you've accumulated a pot worth £454,943. Notice how the jumps get bigger each year until, in the forty-fifth year, your pot grows by a full £26,000. It took nine years to accumulate that much at the beginning, but after 45 years, you're picking that much up each year (on average of course). That's the power of compound interest. The trouble with this is that few of us really have 45 years to play with. If we look at how big our pot will be after 20 or 30 years, things aren't so rosy. Not so rosy at all. The answer is, of course, that if we've got less time to go until retirement, then we have to save a bit harder. Let's say we manage to save at a rate of £400 per month. Again at 5.5 per cent per year, our final pot value will build up like this:

Year	End of year total pot value	Year	End of year total pot value
1	£4,942	2	£10,155
3	£15,656	4	£21,459
5	£27,581	6	£34,040
7	£40,854	8	£48,042
9	£55,627	10	£63,628
11	£72,069	12	£80,975
13	£90,370	14	£100,282
15	£110,740	16	£121,772
17	£133,412	18	£145,691
19	£158,646	20	£172,313
21	£186,732	22	£201,945
23	£217,993	24	£234,925
25	£252,787	26	£271,633
27	£291,514	28	£312,489
29	£334,618	30	£357,964

31	£382,594	32	£408,578
33	£435,992	34	£464,913
35	£495,425	36	£527,616
37	£561,576	38	£597,405
39	£635,204	40	£675,082
41	£716,548	42	£758,429
43	£802,614	44	£849,228
45	£898,407		

By saving £400 per month, we'd get to our figure of £300,000 after about 28 years. Remember that all this is being done in terms of today's money. This means that the £200 or £400 per month that you need to save in 20 years' time is also in today's money. So, you actually have to increase the amount you're saving alongside the average growth in wages each year. That's OK, since your own wages should, we hope, increase at the same rate, enabling you to do this. In reality, what this comes down to is sitting down about once a year and working out, in terms of the then current value of money, how much of it you'll need in retirement. You can then set about working out how much you need to save to get there. If you're doing it right, the amount you save each year should naturally move a little higher as money becomes less valuable.

Of course, we also hope that our wages or salary will actually increase faster than the national average. That's because each year we're gaining more experience and becoming more useful to our employer. If that's the case, then we should be able to increase the amount we save at a rate higher than the average growth in wages. Imagine that our earnings increase at 3 per cent per year faster than the average, and that we therefore increase the amount we save at the same rate. On this basis, starting back at our original £200 per month, our pot would build up like this:

Year	End of year total pot value	Year	End of year total pot value
1	£2,504	2	£5,222
3	£8,166	4	£11,351
5	£14,794	6	£18,511
7	£22,520	8	£26,839
9	£31,487	10	£36,487
11	£41,859	12	£47,628
13	£53,818	14	£60,456
15	£67,569	16	£75,187
17	£83,341	18	£92,065
19	£101,392	20	£111,360
21	£122,008	22	£133,377
23	£145,512	24	£158,457
25	£172,264	26	£186,982
27	£202,667	28	£219,376
29	£237,172	30	£256,118
31	£276,284	32	£297,740
33	£320,565	34	£344,839
35	£370,647	36	£398,079
37	£427,232	38	£458,206
39	£491,108	40	£526,051
41	£563,153	42	£602,541
43	£644,348	44	£688,714
45	£735,788		

That's looking a lot better. At this rate, we could accumulate our pot of £300,000 in about 32 years and we could put ourselves on the Isle of Harris in just 22 years. Not too bad. So even though £200 per month is still a lot to save for many people, we reckon it's a figure you should at least think of as a basic starting point for your saving. Depending on how much retirement income you're aiming for and how long you've got to get your pot together, you might need to save a bit more. Realistically, though, you're unlikely to need a great deal less than about £200 per month unless you really are planning for a very frugal retirement.

Of course, all the above tables are just illustrations. Certainly you're never going to get a steady return, year in year out, from the stock market. As we've said before, it's just that 5.5 per cent is our best guess as to what you can expect over the long term, relative to the growth in what people, on average, are earning. Once you've decided on your best guess, you've no choice but to apply it, year in year out, to your plans. If (and when) things turn out differently from your plan, then you can adjust the plan to suit.

Right, so we have decided equities give us the best home for our money over the long term. (Remember, this is money we are planning on using only when our hair goes grey and we qualify for a bus pass. It is not money that we have to use to pay for the new sofa or anything else of that near-term nature.) But how do we do it? How do we actually go about investing in shares, or 'equities' as we've been calling them?

Is it just a question of choosing a random collection of stocks, or one from each industry or the one being talked about by that nice man in the Sunday papers?

Fortunately, it is a piece of cake these days. You don't even have to know the difference between depreciation, amortisation and flagellation (take it from the Fool: these all amount to pretty much the same thing anyway). Nope, stock market accounting is for the birds. You don't need to stuff around with price-earnings ratios, cash flows, assets, liabilities and all that palaver. This is where you just take a free ride on the conveniently timetabled and excellent value index bus. Forsooth, what a coincidence: here comes one now!

Taking a ride on the index bus

Excuses for being lazy don't come any better than this one. If you haven't already guessed, what we are talking about here are index-tracking funds. Usually shortened to index funds or just plain trackers, these are a type of collective investment that simply aim to track the average performance of the stock market as a whole, by buying all or many of the companies that make up the particular stock market index they are tracking. This is usually either the FTSE 100 index (the one hundred largest companies on the London Stock Exchange) or the FTSE All Share index (roughly the 800 largest companies).

All an index represents is a list of shares chosen for being special in some way. Both the FTSE 100 and the FTSE All Share are 'weighted indices'. This means that the proportion of each share in the index matches the percentage of the index's total value that is made up by that share. Basically it's like a portfolio of shares exactly mimicking the index as a whole. The effect of this is that trackers following these indices closely follow the investment performance of the average pound invested in the UK stock market.

That's it, you just get the average of the stock market's performance (less a bit for charges). Parfait! That's just wonderful, since all the fancy sums we've been doing have been based on the stock market's average performance in the past. So here's something that, without any hassle, can deliver the stock market's average performance in the future, whatever it turns out to be. Above all, a tracker delivers this performance cheaply. That's why we only had to knock 0.5 per cent per year from our 6 per cent expected return from shares. If we'd been investing in the more exotic investment funds, we'd have had to allow an awful lot more than 0.5 per cent per year for charges.

Investing in trackers is easy and is covered in more detail in the *Motley Fool UK Investment Guide* by David Berger. Our website, **www.fool.co.uk**, also has a special section on them, and many others like **www.trackerfunds.com** and **www.trustnet.co.uk** provide plenty of information on all the tracker funds that are available. If you read the Saturday or Sunday newspapers you'll also see some ads for various tracker funds.

In brief, what you're after in a tracker fund is:

● No initial charge.
● Yearly management charge maximum 1 per cent, but preferably no more than 0.5 per cent.
● A five-year history demonstrating that the tracker does indeed do what it says on the tin. In other words, you just want to check that, after taking account of its charges, it does in fact follow the index it's trying to follow.
● The capacity to be sheltered within an Individual Savings Account (more on these later in the chapter).

At the end of June 2000, the 2,132 companies on the London Stock Exchange had a collective value of £1,822,436,000,000. Or, to put it another way, £1.8 trillion. That's a lot of money in anyone's language, even if it is spread around all those different companies. In practice, much of that wealth is made up by the smaller group of large companies (principally the FTSE 100 just referred to). The largest company of all, Vodafone, is itself worth around 10 per cent of the market, and at the time of writing there are another 132 businesses valued at over £2,000 million. These are the companies that most of the funds in trackers are invested in. Even a FTSE All Share tracker may not invest in all of the 800 shares that make up the index, concentrating instead on the larger ones. So long as enough of the biggest companies are covered and the situation is monitored, the tracker should follow its index very closely (before charges).

Typically, tracker funds charge no up-front fee, often known as the bid-offer spread, and will have annual management fees of 0.5 per cent or even less. Contrast that with the other variety of pooled investments in shares, the actively managed funds that claim to give a superior performance. Annual fees for these are generally 1.5 per cent per year or more, and the initial charge might be as much as 6 per cent. Knocking 6 per cent off your funds before they even hit the market, and then taking off another 1.5 per cent per year after that makes a huge difference to the returns you could get over the long term.

But this is the best part. Do you know what these funds do? The ones that claim to give you superior performance? Get this: they don't give you superior performance.

Let's have a look at how tracking the stock market average, the index, and being lower than average in costs works out in terms of real money. *Money Management*, effectively the industry magazine for those in financial services, has performance figures for the unit trusts in the UK All Companies sector. These are the ones that are most closely linked to the fortunes of the UK stock market. They include the UK trackers (although there are only a few of these so they don't really affect things), and the figures can be compared to the average performance (that is, the FTSE All Share). We'll look at the performance of the average fund, the Gartmore UK Index Tracker and the FTSE All Share. The figures show the effect of investing £1,000 (with income reinvested in each case). Going backwards from April 2000 for five and ten years, the performance figures look like this:

Figures for April 2000

	Five-year performance (total of 193 funds)		Ten-year performance (total of 157 funds)	
	Value of £1,000 invested in April 1995	Annual growth rate	Value of £1,000 invested in April 1990	Annual growth rate
Average Fund	£2,164	16.7%	£3,251	12.5%
Gartmore UK Index Tracker	£2,246	17.6%	£3,632	13.8%
FTSE All Share	£2,348	18.6%	£3,881	14.5%

Notice that there are more funds that have been around for five years than there are funds that have been around for ten years (193 against 157). It's interesting to think about why this is. Naturally funds that are doing well tend to stay around. The ones that are doing badly tend not to. They tend to get closed down or absorbed into other funds. These figures therefore exclude, to a large degree, the performance of the very worst funds.

So, we don't like fees and we don't like underperforming investments, but we do like tracker funds. So does one of our regular posters, whose online name is jimsu-san and who posted this message on our index trackers discussion board under the title 'Keep on Trackin':

Hi all,
No doubt some of you will be feeling a bit sore because of the drop in the FOOTSIE and the all share index this past year. Well, that's what you get with a tracker – it tracks! But don't be downhearted, there's no need. By investing in a tracker you've proved yourself to be supremely Foolish.

Speaking personally, I sometimes think it pays to remind myself from time to time why I do things and how I've come to certain decisions in my life. With investments it's so easy to get blown about by prevailing sentiments, either positive or negative, and in order to get things in the correct perspective it's sometimes necessary to reiterate simple truths no matter how familiar we are with them.

I'd like to take some time to explain my supremely Foolish confidence in the index-tracking method of investing. I hope it bolsters your flagging enthusiasm, convinces you if you're on the fence or just generally makes you feel that you can, without any in-depth knowledge, participate profitably in the great global economic expansion that has the potential to enrich us all. Here goes.

The greatest medical minds alive today will tell you that

the two greatest discoveries in medical history are: penicillin and washing hands. *Those same supremely intelligent experts in their fields would also counsel that in order to live a long life you should*: refrain from smoking, eat healthily and fasten your seatbelt when driving. *The moral to this?* **Advice doesn't have to be complicated to be good!** *Every so often I remind myself of this saying because it applies to so many different aspects of life. It is especially true of finance and investing. In fact, this little ditty is so good that it's worth repeating:* **Advice doesn't have to be complicated to be good**.

Investing in an index-tracking fund will enable you to beat, more or less, 90 per cent of actively managed funds over the long term and with little or no effort on your part. Here's why and how.

Investment Management, as traditionally practised, is based on the single premise that: professional investment managers CAN beat the market. This premise, as we enter 2001 appears to be built on sand.

Up to about 1960, 90 per cent of all stock exchange activity was carried out by individuals. The remaining 10 per cent was carried out by institutions. In those laid-back days it was relatively easy for the institutions to beat the market because they had so many more targets of opportunity. Because they were competing, predominantly, with individuals who had far less in the way of expertise at their disposal, the chances of gaining the upper hand and hence enjoying superior returns were greatly enhanced.

Today the opposite is true. The institutions now constitute 90 per cent of buying and selling of shares and individuals account for only 10 per cent. What can we therefore draw from this? The first thing to note is that instead of the institutions playing the market, the institutions themselves indeed now constitute the market. *The second thing to deduce from this is the fact that if the institutions are the market then in attempting to get the upper hand they are trying to beat themselves.*

The active investment manager, unlike in the '60s, is no longer competing with amateurs, cautious and out of touch with the market. Instead, he is competing with other equally competent experts, all of whom have access to the same technology, information and ultra-fast and efficient decision-making processes.

In the present day this is a huge game. In the USA, at least 200 major institutional investors together with 1,000 or so small- and medium-sized institutions buy and sell to each other each day and every day. All trying to outdo each other, all trying to find a chink in the others' armoury. These institutions are not driven by long-term performance as they should be, but rather by short-term sales targets, bonus payments and career aspirations.

As the game has changed so much over the last forty years or so, what must the active fund manager now do to cover the costs of active fund management? Quite a lot actually. Institutions hold stocks for typically 15–18 months. Let's assume, as an example, that the fund carries an annual operating cost of 3 per cent (made up of buying and selling and active management costs). Also let's assume an average market annual rate of return of 10 per cent. In order to only match the market's rate of return in this instance, the active manager must return 13 per cent before costs. Put another way, the manager must be able to outperform the market by 30 per cent in order to merely match that same market.

Bearing in mind the previously stated facts, that these guys are fiercely competing with each other, then is it any wonder that over the long term the vast majority of active fund managers fail to even equal the market, never mind beat it?

Some pundits will tell you that active fund managers do beat the market and yes, this is true. However, this success needs to be seen in context. Every year some professionals will beat their fellow professionals. Even over a decade a few will come out top. The problem with trying to identify these rare creatures is the fact that past performance is hopeless as a guide to the future. In fact, records show that the managers who have done well in the past are less likely to do well in the future. Regression to the mean is a very powerful force in investing.

So many of these professionals are now so good that it makes it nearly impossible for any one of them or group of them to outperform the market that they themselves now constitute.

The answer to all of this complication and worry is simple. Just like the greatest medical discoveries being penicillin and washing hands, the greatest investment that would suit the majority of people is the humble Powerful Plodder *as it's known in the States, or as we call it, the index tracking fund.*

When you think about it, being able to keep pace with stock market returns and hence placing yourself in the top 10–15 per cent of investors over the long term with no hassle, minimum costs and no effort has got to be extremely Foolish.

Forgive me if I've covered ground you're only too aware of, but sometimes, especially after a year when the index went down, it doesn't do any harm at all just to restate and emphasize certain simple, basic truths concerning the investment scene.

Kind regards
Jim

A regular contribution into a tracker fund over a period of many years will gradually build into a very nice nest egg. You don't need to be a professional to invest in one and it won't take oodles of your time. In fact, you've almost cracked investing for your retirement (yes, and we're only on Chapter 3, so what's the rest of the book about?). All you really have to do now is read the bit about ISAs.

Investing in individual shares

Well, how about it? Share selection by private investors is becoming more and more popular. The growing number of online execution-only stockbrokers has made buying and selling shares as easy as clicking a mouse, and very cheap, too. That technical ease has been matched by a wide range of information sources that are now available to those with access to the Internet. Companies are now posting their results on their own websites as they are released. This means the private investor gets the data at the same time as the professional investor. In addition to this, specialized data providers all have data online, and usually it is free. Respected names like Bloomberg, Reuters and the *Financial Times* all have excellent websites devoted to bringing up-to-date information to the small investor. More recently, we have seen the advent of TV channels devoted to finance. Bloomberg TV is well established and has been joined by newcomers such as The Money Channel and Simply Money. There's even the jolly old

Motley Fool in the playing field. The Internet has brought about a revolution in information sources available to the private investor.

If this subject interests you at all, stop by some of these sources and see what you think. If you want to go further, do, but don't feel compelled to do so. Investing in individual shares isn't for everybody; in fact it's only for the minority who want to try and do better than the index and think they can. Our website and some of our other books deal with the subject. It's not something we want to go into in any depth here, and if you have no real interest in it and just want to sort out something simple to take you through to your retirement, then forget we ever mentioned it.

We talk a little more about investing in a particular type of individual shares, those that provide income, in Chapter 6, The Endlessly Replenishing Retirement Portfolio.

Individual Savings Accounts: designed to be simple

But in fact outrageously complicated. Individual Savings Accounts (ISAs) have actually been a running joke here at the Motley Fool. You see, they are so complicated that we have tried to explain them in simple terms quite a few times now (on our website, in our books and elsewhere), but have mostly failed. One of the Motley Fool's personal finance writers was actually hired partly because she *could* explain ISAs pretty well.

This is all a bit sad, because ISAs are a great invention. Therefore, instead of attempting my own explanation of them, possibly confusing you and thereby putting you off altogether, which would be a tragedy, I'm going to crib. Much of what follows in this section and the accompanying section (especially the brilliant bit about teapots) has been lifted wholesale from the *Motley Fool UK Investment Guide* with absolutely zero regard for copyright, intellectual integrity, honesty or anything else honourable or decent. In turn, the *Investment Guide* lifted much of it from the new personal finance writer we just mentioned, who did the best job of explaining them. We don't care! We just want you to understand about ISAs. They're that important. Remember, we're doing this for you.

An ISA allows anyone to invest up to £7,000 a year into the stock market, and all subsequent gains are free of capital gains tax. There is also a concession on dividends[1] although it is not worth as much as it used to be and will fade away by 2004. Nevertheless, the total freedom of not having to worry about capital gains tax, a tax in which the government can take up to 40 per cent of your investment's growth above a yearly allowance (currently a bit over £7,000), makes these little beauties very attractive indeed.

When you buy an index tracker (or an underperforming managed fund), you can generally buy it pre-wrapped in an ISA. The nice thing about doing this is that the manager of the index tracker will typically throw in the ISA wrapper for free, keeping your costs down.

Alternatively, you can buy your own ISA wrapper (called a 'self-select ISA') and put what you like into it yourself. The trouble with this is that you'll have to pay for the ISA and then pay for what you put into it on top. For this reason, self-select ISAs tend to be used only

---

[1] Dividends are money paid twice a year by some companies to their shareholders

where you are putting shares directly into the ISA, since, with the big exception of dealing charges when you buy and sell, shares have no additional ongoing costs.

Once you've got your money in an ISA, not only will your investment gains never be subject to capital gains tax; you won't get charged any income tax on interest received on it, and you won't incur any tax when you take money out of it, either. Unfortunately, as ever, the devil is in the detail. Thankfully, for once, the detail does nothing to reduce (or, for that matter, improve) the usefulness of the product. It serves only to make the head a bit sore. So as to prevent our heads from getting sore and trying not to interrupt the flow of thought in the book, all the detailed stuff you need to know about ISAs is in the accompanying section, including the bizarre teapot analogy. Feel free to consult it as and when you need to.

For now, though, all you need to know is that an index tracker, cocooned within the tax-proof shelter of an ISA, represents a fine way to save over the long term for your retirement.

ISA detail: Maxis, Minis and CATs

There are two basic types of ISA: the Maxi-ISA and the Mini-ISA. It's pretty important to be clear about the differences because, in each tax year, you are allowed (assuming that you're a UK resident aged 18 or over) to invest in just one of the two types. Each type has three separate components: cash, stocks and shares, and insurance. The difference between the two is that in the Maxi, they're all mushed together into the same account, whereas with the Mini, each of the bits are in different accounts. It's perhaps easiest to think of the Maxi as being like one big teapot into which you can put up to three different types of teabag (that is, one teabag for cash, one teabag for stocks and shares and one teabag for insurance). Since it's all in one teapot, only one person can be mother. In other words, you have to pick one financial organization to run the whole Maxi-ISA for you.

Similarly, you can think of the Mini-ISA as being like three small teapots, each of which can contain a different teabag (except you can't have the same type of teabag in two different pots). So, if you like the interest rates on someone's cash Mini-ISA, but you don't like the charges on their stocks and shares Mini-ISA, then you can open the cash Mini with them, but go to someone else for the stocks and shares Mini. Before we leave our teapots, we should just say that we don't much like the taste of insurance teabags. We don't like the confusion between insurance and investment at the best of times and we really can't work out who would want to put insurance policies into an ISA. It looks like we're not the only ones. Very few financial organizations offer them and, according to the government, in the first nine months of the ISA only £44 million had been put into the insurance component compared to more than £17 billion into cash and stocks and shares. Really, then, we'd say that you can simplify matters greatly by just ignoring the insurance component and concentrating on the other bits.

Now we've got the difference between these Maxis and Minis sorted out, let's have a look at the annual limits. For the 2000/2001 tax year, and for the next five years, you can invest up to £7,000 in a Maxi-ISA.

You can put as much of this into the stocks and shares component as you like, but you can only put up to £3,000 into the cash component. For Mini-ISAs, the limits are £3,000 for a stocks and shares Mini and £3,000 for a cash Mini this tax year, and for the next five years.

Each new tax year brings the opportunity to make fresh subscriptions to an existing ISA, or to open a whole new ISA. Of course, if you keep opening a new ISA each year, things are going to get pretty complicated. To simplify matters, transfers from one ISA into another are allowed. However, the components must remain the same. So, once you've gone for the stocks and shares component of a Maxi-ISA or a stocks and shares Mini, you can move it around all over the place, but it must always remain in stocks and shares. Similarly, when you've gone for a cash component, it must always stay in cash. Any transfers like this do not count for the purposes of each year's allowances.

As you can probably imagine, you can only really put cash (and one or two things that are very like cash) into a cash ISA. The fun starts when you get to the stocks and shares bit. Here you can put in most of the things that you might want to. You can put shares in it, so long as they're quoted on a major stock exchange, you can put most unit trusts and investment trusts into it and you can put gilts and corporate bonds into it. You can even hold a bit of cash in it, but this must be for the purpose of buying the other investments that we've just mentioned. You can't hold cash in a stocks and shares component 'for the sole purpose of sheltering interest on cash deposits from tax'.

The government has designed a scheme to help

people tell which ISAs meet certain minimum standards. It's designed to reassure us a bit and it does just that. It's a voluntary code and it in no way guarantees returns, but if an ISA is CAT-marked, it does tell you that certain conditions are met. CAT stands for Charges, Access and Terms, the three areas that the standards cover. For Charges, the provisions are that cash ISAs can make no charge at all, and stocks and shares ISAs can only charge up to 1 per cent of the value of the ISA per year. For Access, you've got to be able to get at your money within seven working days. The most important part of the Terms bit is that the interest rate on cash ISAs can't be more than 2 per cent below the base rate, at least 50 per cent of stocks and shares ISAs must be invested in Europe and units must have the same buying and selling price.

How you get that much

Having started this chapter with a question ('How do you get that much?'), it would be a bit sad if we were unable to finish it with an answer. Thankfully, we can. Summarizing what we have learnt so far, here's how you get that much:

- Invest steadily in the stock market over the long term.
- Increase the amount you're saving over the years alongside the amount you're earning.
- Probably the most simple and effective way to invest in the stock market is via an index tracker.
- Pay close attention to charges.

- Shelter your investment within an ISA.

That's it. You could put the book down at this point, knowing all you need to know to fund your retirement. You might be the curious type, though, and are wondering where pensions fit in, what an annuity is, how you could retire earlier, what to do about your house, what to do when you finally get to retirement and a whole lot more. If that's so – and if you've read this far I'm guessing it probably is – you should read on, because there is bags of fun stuff to come. (OK, it's not exactly fun, but it is quite useful.)

Chapter 4
Pensions: The Good, the Bad and the Ugly

The sweet simplicity of the three per cents.
Benjamin Disraeli

How many times have you heard people say: 'I really must do something about my pension, but I don't understand a word my financial adviser says.' Maybe you've said it yourself. Generally, the conversation stops there, accompanied by uncomfortable downward glances, shoe shuffling, a general feeling of unease and mutterings along the lines of 'Gosh, it's so hard to know, isn't it? I mean, I just don't understand all that stuff…'

It's a shame alright, but it's not surprising that people don't discuss their pensions, as they have never received any education about them, they find the whole subject intimidating in the extreme and the last thing the professionals would like is for people to be considering these investments from a knowledgeable standpoint. Just why this is, we are about to see.

You've got to have a pension, haven't you?

Well, yes, and then again, no. Before we answer this in a slightly more helpful manner, let's take a quick look at what pensions actually are. If you already have a pension yourself, our guess is that you'll be quite interested to hear what we have to say in this chapter. If you don't yet have one, then we hope it will also provide some food for thought, because sure as goldfish swim, the Pope is Catholic and the Shipping Forecast must mean something to someone somewhere, there is a financial adviser out there who is going to try and sell you one of these. Soon.

What is a pension?

'What is life?' 'Does s/he love me?' 'Will it pass the MOT?' We've all probably asked ourselves one or more of these questions at some point in our lives. How many times, though, have you looked up at the unimaginably distant haze of the Milky Way, with a shooting star blazing its trail of light across the heavens, and asked yourself that whimsical and age-old question: 'What exactly *is* a pension?'

A pension is an income that you receive after you've stopped work. To build up a big enough pot of money to provide that income, someone has to do some saving. What makes one pension scheme different from another is down to how this money is saved, who it is saved by and how the income is eventually generated.

The thing is, pensions were simple once. When Gladstone was Chancellor (that was back in the nineteenth century for anyone like me who never paid attention during history and is now too embarrassed to admit their appalling ignorance), all you had to do was buy some of his sweet 3 per cent Consol gilts, secure in the knowledge that the interest from these would keep you going happily for the rest of your natural days. Nowadays, a combination of meddling politicians less able than him, inflation, tax, rising populations and a greedy financial services industry has combined to make this whole area a confusing jungle. Still, that's life and the good news is you don't have to know as much about it as you probably think you do, and that the underlying concepts aren't too hard to grasp.

The key attraction of pensions nowadays is that, in order to encourage us to save for our retirement, the government provides a tax break. So long as a pension scheme fulfils the criteria they have set down, then the money that goes into it comes out of your *pre-tax* earnings. Think of it this way: you put some money in, then the government chips in the tax that you have paid (or would pay) on that money. These contributions form a pension fund, which is invested over the years until your retirement. In theory all this seems dandy. In practice, life is once again about to take a shot across your bows. There are (more than) a few complications along the way.

We're going to take a look at the state pension, occupational pensions and private pensions (commonly known as personal pension plans or PPPs).

The State Pension

The state pension scheme basically comes in two bits – the 'basic pension' and the 'State Earnings-Related Pension Scheme' (SERPS).

Basic Pension

Its value is slowly being whittled away, as we saw in Chapter 1. Slipping in a 2 per cent drop in growth was a shrewd manoeuvre by the Thatcher government in 1981. The Tories, in the aftermath of their 1979 landslide, realized that, since there was no investment fund out of which pensions were being paid (they are paid by the National Insurance contributions of those currently working), the rapidly ageing population was going to mean that pensions at the current levels were going to become too expensive. They therefore cut the rate at which pensions appreciated and so hastened the stranglehold on this country's old people. Whatever you think of the rights and wrongs of this, it is the case that by the time many people reading this book retire, they'll be lucky if the weekly state pension buys them a bottle of blue hair rinse and a packet of Mr Kipling's jam tarts. It's also worth bearing in mind that not everybody qualifies for it — you have to have made a minimum level of National Insurance contributions (roughly speaking, you'll be OK if you've earned at least the same amount as the basic pension for most of your working life).

One other thing that is worth mentioning at this stage is the Minimum Income Guarantee or 'MIG'. This effectively sets a floor to the amount of income a retired person can get. From April 2001, the MIG will amount to £92.15, about £20 more than the basic state pension. However, once other sources of income take you past the MIG, then all you get is the state pension, plus any entitlement to SERPS.

SERPS and 'contracting out'

The basic pension replaces your lowest slice of income (that is, up to £72.50 per week from April, 2001). The State Earnings-Related Pension Scheme (SERPS) is designed to replace your income from £72 per week to £500 per week. It is 'earnings-related' because the more you earn (up to £500), the greater your National Insurance contributions and the more SERPS you get. However, as you go from £72 to £500, less and less of your income is actually replaced. This means that someone earning, say, £200 per week will retire on a higher percentage of their pre-retirement income than someone who was earning £500 per week (although they will, of course, get less actual money). Income above the £500 per week level does not get replaced under SERPS and the scheme is only available for employees, not the self-employed.

If you want, you can choose to opt out of SERPS. This is called 'contracting out'. The effect of this is that your National Insurance payments, which would have gone towards providing your SERPS benefits, instead get paid into your occupational or personal pension. Your pension scheme then guarantees to pay out at least the SERPS benefits that you have given up. Basically, all you are doing is replacing SERPS with your own arrangements. Whether or not to contract out of SERPS is a tricky question, which depends on your view of future investment returns. One thing to remember is that SERPS is basically a form of defined benefit pension. Contracting out in favour of a defined contribution pension, therefore, carries risk. (Don't worry, we'll talk about this 'defined' business in the next section, 'Occupational pension schemes'.) As with any situation where you are taking extra risk in the hope of greater returns, the longer you have for it to come good, the better. Contracting out is therefore likely to make more sense the younger you are.

Occupational pension schemes

Forty years on the shop floor at Harding and Sedgewick ends with a handshake, a carriage clock and a generous pension to reflect the hard work and faithful service of a lifetime:

> *'Thank you, Higgins. Any plans for the future, my man?'*
>
> *'Well, sir, there's an allotment to dig and the cricket to watch. And may I say what a fine company this has been to work for over the years and what gentlemen you and your father before you have been. It has been an honour to work my fingers to the bone fourteen hours a day for a pittance of a weekly wage and a five shilling bonus every other Christmas. The outstanding growth in your personal wealth over that time and the way in which I was allowed to shine your shoes on my birthday have been a source of great pride to me. Truly a privilege, sir. Thank 'ee.'*

Yes, those were the days, the days of Mrs Miniver and Morris Eights, of the Movietone News and good old British honesty and pluck and people jolly well knowing their place. Nowadays, though, an employee with a full company pension is about as common as rocking horse manure. Frank Field, the MP who is an expert on pensions (and, you may remember, got sacked from the government for his troubles), reckons that only 1 per cent of the population are entitled to one. In these days of corporate restructuring and takeovers, few of us have the luxury of staying with one company for the whole of our working lives.

Even so, occupational pensions can provide the basis

for a sound retirement income and should generally be opted *for* rather than against. As often seems to be the case, it's just that the picture is a bit more complicated than it was back then, when the sun always shone in June and we knew with such certainty who the baddies were.

The best occupational pensions are to be found in the public sector. If you are in the police force, your pension will be generous indeed and will be paid for out of the organization's budget, not an investment fund. Elsewhere, though, and especially in the private sector, pensions are paid out of an investment fund into which both employee and employer contribute. This fund will be invested in a variety of things, although generally it is heavily weighted into equities. That said, the equity investments are more likely to take the form of the underperforming unit trusts we've already talked about. There are two basic types of occupational pension scheme: defined benefit and defined contribution.

We're already getting into jargon here with 'defined benefit' and 'defined contribution', but all this boils down to is who takes the risk of the investments not performing well enough. Having an idea of who takes the risk is something well worth knowing. With a *defined benefit* pension scheme, the final benefit is what 'defines' how much the policy is worth. In effect, the final benefit – aka 'how much you get' – is guaranteed. Typically, your eventual benefits from this type of scheme are defined as a proportion of your final salary and they are often referred to as 'final salary' schemes for this reason. With these pensions, your retirement income (and any lump sum that you stand to get) simply comes out of the total pension pot that your employer has been building up over the years for all employees. If the investments have performed badly and there isn't enough in the pot, then your employer has to stump up the difference. Of course, if the investments have performed well and there is extra in the pot, then the employer often gets to keep the extra. (There's always a pay-off for taking risk, right?)

In a *defined contribution* pension, the value of the policy is defined by what is put into it. For this reason, they are sometimes known as 'money purchase schemes'. The level of your final benefits also depends on how well the investments in your scheme perform, and they are therefore not guaranteed. If the investments perform well, then you will get the extra benefit. However, if performance is poor, then you'll end up with a lower retirement income than you were hoping for. In this case, it's you that takes the risk, not your employer.

Defined benefit occupational schemes

As we've just seen, defined benefit occupational schemes pay you benefits based on your final salary (or, perhaps, an average of your salary for the last few years of your employment). Typically, the benefits will involve a lump sum and an income for life. There may well be a number of useful frills, such as life insurance and a pension for your spouse if they survive you.

The lump sum and income are generally expressed as a fraction of your final salary per year of service. Imagine that you are getting retirement income of $\frac{1}{60}$ of your final salary and a lump sum of $\frac{3}{80}$ of your final salary per year of service, and you have 20 years of service. You will stand to receive ⅓ (that is, $^{20}/_{60}$) of your final salary as income and ¾ (that is, $^{60}/_{80}$) of your final salary as a lump sum.

Defined benefit schemes are generally pretty attractive because your employer takes the risk of things not working out on the investment front. Unfortunately, this fact is not lost on most employers and they are stampeding to change to the next option.

Defined contribution occupational schemes

The effect of a defined contribution occupational scheme is similar to having a personal pension (which we're coming to next) into which your employer makes contributions. Your benefits depend on what is put into it and how the investments perform. At retirement you get a tax-free lump sum and the remainder of your fund must be used to purchase something called an annuity (which we'll come to in the next chapter). How much of the fund you can take out as tax-free cash depends on final salary and length of service.

Some schemes offer you a choice of how much to put in. For example, your employer may offer to match the amount you put into the pension by contributing the same amount again. However, just because your employer has offered to put money into a pension scheme if you do, it doesn't necessarily mean that you should. It really depends on the level of the contributions. If your employer offers to match your contributions (or better), then it would almost certainly make sense to take it. However, if your employer only puts in, say, £1 for every £9 that you put in, then the decision would be more difficult: other factors about whether or not to opt for the pension will probably be more relevant.

Preserved benefits and transfers

Under an occupational scheme, if you have worked for an employer for two years, you get to keep the value of any pensions benefits that have built up if you change jobs. Either you can keep the 'preserved benefits' in the old scheme, or you can get the old scheme to transfer enough money (called the 'transfer value') to the new scheme to give you the same benefits that you had already built up in the old scheme. The trouble with transferring is that it often costs you money to do it. If you have worked for less than two years with an employer, you basically just get back any contributions that you've put in.

AVCs and FSAVCs

This is an option for people who are members of an occupational scheme, but who don't think their benefits are going to be enough. An AVC scheme is run by the employer to enable people to top their pension contributions up to the maximum allowed. AVC stands for Additional Voluntary Contribution. Where your employer does not offer an AVC scheme (or even if they do, but we'll come to that), you can contribute to an FSAVC scheme (which stands for Free-Standing AVC).

As you might imagine, an AVC (or FSAVC) for a defined contribution pension just increases your contributions, although they might be in a slightly different place from your main scheme. Where an AVC scheme is available for a defined benefit pension scheme (generally only in the public sector), your contributions can purchase 'added years'. In other words, you are buying extra years to be taken into account in calculating your final salary benefits.

An AVC, sponsored by your employer, has an advantage over an FSAVC because of 'economies of scale'. In other words, by grouping together with your fellow employees, the overall charges tend to be lower. FSAVCs are very similar to the personal pension plans we're shortly going to hear about. They generally have similar, punitive charging structures, your fund will be channelled into the same kinds of underperforming investments and they are sold by the same people. Take a look at this quote from an article in the *Financial Times* of 25 April 1998:

> *Bacon & Woodrow, one of the biggest pension analysts, warned recently that the stand-alone alternative to company-sponsored AVCs – free-standing AVCs (FSAVCs) – is being sold inappropriately.*
>
> *Indeed, B&W said this week that about a quarter of pension schemes contained members who had paid commission to a salesperson, only to end up with an FSAVC identical to the in-house AVC – except for higher charges to cover the commission.*

It comes as no great surprise, then, that the Financial Services Authority (FSA) has launched a review into FSAVCs sold between April 1988 and August 1999. At the moment, the review is focusing on sales of FSAVCs where it has meant that the investor missed out on possible employer contributions to an available AVC scheme. But, given the way that the review of mis-selling into personal pensions has gone (don't worry, we're getting there), who knows where this may end up. In February 2000, the FSA estimated that compensation payable to investors will be between £95 million and £200 million. Anyway, the bottom line on this is that, if you have an occupational pension scheme and want to top up your contributions, an in-house AVC scheme is likely to be a far more attractive option than a FSAVC scheme.

Who puts the money in

One final thing to think about with an occupational pension is who puts the money in. In a pension scheme offered by your employer, you might put a bit in each month and so might your employer. Sounds good, but let's think of it in another way. You, as an employee, are worth a certain amount to your employer and (so long as you, and/or your union, make the right noises when your pay is reviewed) hopefully this is the amount that you are paid. It makes little difference to your employer whether all your benefits come in the form of your salary or whether your salary is 5 per cent less and he pays 5 per cent into a pensions scheme for you. What matters is your overall package. If your employer offers what is generally considered to be an attractive pension scheme, then ask yourself how much more salary you could be paid if you didn't take the pension. Of course, much of this is fairly academic since few of us actually have that much control over our benefits package. Still, it's as well to think about things in this way. It helps keep the mind focused and that's what much of this book is really about.

Good and bad

Taking into account the previous section and reckoning that we don't have the option to take our employer's contribution to our occupational scheme in the form of extra salary or a tube of Smarties on our desk every morning, what makes occupational pension schemes attractive is that contribution from the employer. What makes them less attractive is the fact that they're not very portable. Since you are unlikely, these days, to be spending the whole forty years of your career at Harding and Sedgewick – the average person changes job five times in their working lives and less than 5 per cent of men and 1 per cent of women stay in the same job for thirty years – this could leave you with a number of small pensions, each paying out not very much. If it is portable, you're still likely to lose out to some extent.

There are good things, then, and bad things about company pension schemes. As throughout this book, we don't seek to tell you what you should do and what you shouldn't do – that would be pointless; what we seek to do is give you the information to make informed decisions on your own behalf. What we hope you will take away from this short section is that, for most people, an occupational pension is probably not going to provide the single, all-encompassing answer to a prosperous dotage.

Avanti!

Personal pension plans

The late 1980s. Thatcher's generation of self-employed entrepreneurs is busily engaged by turns in quaffing lager, racing around in a Ford Escort XR3i and revolu-

tionizing the British economy, but none of them, of
course, has access to an occupational pension scheme.
We have to presume this didn't please the boss and following a gentle word in the ear of Nigel Lawson, the
Chancellor of the time, an acronym was born:

> 'Unfair, Nigel! These are my children. Go and DO
> something about it!' roars the 'T', eyes ablaze with fury
> and index finger pointing to the door of the Cabinet
> Room.
> 'Immediately, Ma'am,' ripostes Mr Lawson and scur-
> ries off to do the Leaderene's bidding.

PPPs, or personal pension plans, give self-employed people, or those working for small businesses without occupational schemes, a crack – as they like to say in the
Sunday newspapers – of the pensions whip. They are
defined contribution schemes into which the PPP holder
can pay up to a maximum percentage of their income
(rising from a maximum of 17.5 per cent at the age of
thirty-five or below to 40 per cent at the age of sixty or
above). These payments then go into an investment
fund, run by an investment or insurance company, into
which the government also contributes the tax the
investor would have paid. In other words, they get *tax
relief* on their contributions, an undoubted advantage.
The fund grows and then, on retirement, you can take
25 per cent of your fund as a lump sum and the remainder is used to buy something called an annuity to provide an income. Simple? No, definitely not.

First, it was with PPPs that the financial professionals
got their knickers in a very painful twist in the late 1980s
and early 1990s. By encouraging people to purchase

their (expensive) plans and to abandon the perfectly good occupational schemes many of them were already in, they were giving disastrous financial advice, which would leave most of these people at a financial disadvantage in years to come. This has become known as the 'Pensions mis-selling scandal' and the precise reasons it arose (the companies involved were making a killing from selling these policies) will become painfully obvious as we consider the issue of investment charges in just one short paragraph from here. Suffice to say that some of the biggest names in financial services were implicated to the tune of billions of pounds of compensation, which they are now having to pay to those they disadvantaged by their phoney advice. The issue was supposed to be in the process of being resolved in early 1998 (with some judicious prodding from Parliament and fines for those who were reluctant to pay compensation), when it all hit centre stage again. The government decreed in February of that year that the companies would have to investigate another 1.5 *million* cases, pushing the likely compensation bill from £5,000 million to beyond £11,000 million at a single stroke. The minister responsible referred to this as 'an awful lot of money' and we're with him on that one.

Next comes the thorny issue of charges. Let's cast our minds back for a moment to the previous chapter, where we looked at compound interest. We saw how important it was, nay vital, to start on the investing trail as early as possible. Time and patience are the friends of the Foolish investor. What think you, then, Fool, of giving up 80 per cent or more of your first two years' contributions to a PPP in charges? This is money that will not go into your future, but into someone else's, either the financial adviser who sold you the plan, who takes it as his commission, or else the investment company itself. That's 80 per cent or more of the first two *paramount* years: also an awful lot of very important money. The process by which this money is taken from investors is called front-end loading and it's as bad for investors as it is good for the people selling the pension policies. (And are you still with us here?) It gets worse, breathtakingly so. Often, if you change the amount of your contributions, the company will *restart* the punitive charges schedule. Look at this e-mail from David Carter in 1998:

> *I increased my contribution to £300 [from £100] per month with effect from May 1st 1998. Then came the shock disclosure and here I do quote, because I was flabbergasted when I saw:*
> *'HOW MUCH WILL THE ADVICE COST?*
> *'Company X will provide services and remuneration for arranging and servicing this increase [sic] to your plan amounting to £77.11 per month on average in the first year and a variable amount per month thereafter, being for example £64.50 on average in the second year, £15.28 in the third year and £24.28 in the final year. These amounts have been included in the deductions shown above and are determined by the size of the con- tribution increase and payment term.'*
> *Now, I've never been much of a jargon man myself. But to my simple thinking, this all adds up to a total of £2,200 over four years just to service an increase to my premium – I even had to write the letter authorizing the increase to the company direct debit!*
> *I rang my Company X salesman (I've never accepted their term of 'advisor') who I've known for thirteen*

years. He was upset that I should question this 25 per cent (averaged over 4 years) charge. He compared it to my fees for recruiting staff for my clients (average: 20 per cent of first year's remuneration). I respectfully pointed out to him that I don't make any charges when a client increases someone's salary! (Anyway, isn't the first year's fee 40 per cent?)

He's coming to see me tomorrow to try and sort it out. He asked me to find out whether other pension providers charge less – probably so that he can show me how well the Company X investment out-performs any other that I might choose. I don't want to play that game and told him that I shall not be doing any business with Company X again.

Sadly, what happened to David happens to many people with personal pensions who think they're saving more and more for the future. Each time they increase their contributions, they don't realize they are paying directly into the pockets of the people who are running their policy.

Now, interesting things also happen when you stop paying into your personal pension plan earlier than you'd planned. There could be a variety of reasons for this, which were nicely detailed in an article in the *Independent* on 15 November 1997: Lincoln, a PPP provider, found that 45 per cent (!) of its pension premiums lapse within three years and, to their credit, commissioned research into why this was so. This research revealed that 34 per cent lapsed due to unemployment, 23 per cent due to career breaks to raise a child and 20 per cent because people were offered a good occupational scheme – in other words 77 per cent of lapses were due to perfectly acceptable reasons, not just people jibbing out for no reason.

Let's turn to the pages of *Money Management*, the magazine of choice for the financial services industry. The November 1997 edition had some interesting intelligence and, in this instance, *MM* did a pretty good hatchet job of its own on our behalf.

Brace yourselves for the riveting story behind the paid-up value and the transfer value. If you decide to stop paying into your PPP, you can do one of two things: leave the money where it is or transfer it out. If you transfer it elsewhere you get (no great surprises here) the transfer value. If you leave it where it is, the company will credit you with a paid-up value that will then grow until the end of the term and you can take whatever benefits might be coming your way. So far, so good, but you won't be surprised to hear that some of the transfer values were truly appalling. Consider the case of a thirty-year PPP with J. Rothschild Assurance, in which contributions of £200 per month were stopped after two years. Now, um, 24 x 200 equals, um, 4,800, right? No, that can't be right, let's check it again, 24 x 200 equals ...

(Sounds of head-scratching, whistling, pencil scribbling through long multiplication sums)

... um, yes, 4,800.

Now, in this case, the transfer value of the fund after two years is actually only £1,473 – in other words 69 per cent *lower* than the contributions paid in. Just 69 per cent depreciation in two years: now, that's investment!

Fair enough, you might say (we wouldn't), they have to penalize people who decide to leave early, but take a look at their paid-up value: that's a whopping £4,788. This is just about what you've paid in contributions and a definite incentive to leave the money where it is, rather than transfer it elsewhere. Not bad, you might think (we wouldn't): zero growth after two years. Leave it there and it'll grow nicely, you might think. Wrong! If we then move on to the maturity value of this £4,788 at thirty years, we see that it is only £13,826, or equivalent to a paltry return of around 4 per cent per year.

Now, picture for a moment having had the misfortune of being sweet-talked into a Rothschild plan that you found you had to leave for one reason or another. The consequences are nothing short of catastrophic. For you, anyway. However, someone, somewhere, is getting the benefit of all that compound interest on 4,800 minus 1,473, or £3,327 over thirty years. Nice work if you can get it, we say.

We'd like to give this as an isolated example, but it isn't. In fact, let's take a look at Lincoln itself, which commissioned the study into PPP lapses: both the two-year transfer and paid-up values of their thirty-year policies were a meagre £1,346, less even than Rothschild. Now reckon that it's not just the odd person here or there who is getting hammered by these poor transfer values – according to the July 1998 edition of *Money Management*, as many as 40 per cent of pension plan-holders end up cancelling their contracts within five years, often as a result of what they describe as 'overzealous' selling by financial advisers.

When talking about charges, it can also be helpful to look at the effect of charges by the amount of pence in each contributed pound they eat up. This table has been taken from an article in *Money Management* in 1992, entitled 'Expenses and the Impact of Disclosure' and we think it speaks for itself:

Effect of charges on each pound paid into personal pension plans

	10 yrs	25 yrs
Lowest	10p	13p
Median	17p	20p
Highest	29p	31p

Numbers like these leave us with difficulty in believing that the professionals have our best interests at heart, and little has changed since 1992. In a July 1998 survey of the cost of charges, *Money Management* still found they had a huge impact, with our old friend, Lincoln, topping the bill at a cost of a whisker under £20,000 on a 25-year policy with contributions of £200 per month. In other words, the charges amounted to almost exactly one third of the total contributions! The last sentence of the November 1997 *MM* article sums it all up nicely:

> *No wonder the public places such little trust in the industry.*

Couldn't have put it better ourselves.

We're not finished, unfortunately, because even when investors arrive at a stage where their contributions are actually being invested in something that earns money, they don't have a great deal of say over just what those investments are. The contributions will generally be into one of the underperforming unit trusts that we heard about in Chapter 3, and the best the punters can hope for is to choose between the unit trusts on offer by the pension plan provider.

By now, we hope you've worked out that one of the

biggest problems that we have with defined contribution pensions is that they tend to cost too much. Being products which are designed to produce money, costing too much is a major failing. There are, of course, one or two other problems, like the fact that the tax relief isn't quite what it's cracked up to be, as we'll see in a moment, and that you end up having to buy a nasty annuity which we discuss in the next chapter. Still, if you can keep your charges down, then pensions begin to look a fair bit more attractive. This brings us back to the subject of index trackers.

Foolish Pension Options

Index Tracking Pensions

Pensions and ISAs and what have you are just wrappers for your underlying investments. Think of them as financial clingfilm. Clingfilm does not change what's inside, merely the effect of the outside world on it. If the contents are good, like a slice of mature farmhouse cheddar, they stay good. If the contents are bad, like four-day-old fish pie, then they stay that way. So, just as a nice, tasty, low-cost index tracker is likely to outperform the majority of other investments when wrapped up in an ISA, it's likely to do the same thing when wrapped up inside a pension. You will, of course, have to end up spending most of the money on an annuity. Talking of which, you should make sure that the pension doesn't penalize you for buying the annuity from a different provider. Annuities can vary hugely in terms of value and it is always worth shopping around for the best deal.

But what if you're in an occupational pension scheme and decide you want to transfer your retirement funds into an index tracker? Well, if you're in a final salary (that is, defined benefit) scheme, you simply can't. In that case you have no say over where or how your money is invested and it's pretty well irrelevant to you anyway, since no matter how well the investments perform, your pension is fixed as a percentage of your final salary. On the other hand, if you're in a money purchase or defined contribution scheme, then an index tracker may be one of the places into which you can invest your money, in which case that's great. If it isn't one of the options, then there's no harm in writing to the scheme manager asking why not.

Stakeholder pensions

The much-talked-about 'stakeholder pensions' will be available from April 2001 and they look as though they will be relatively attractive. Employers (with more than five employees) will have to make a stakeholder scheme available unless they are making contributions, on behalf of their employees, of 3 per cent of salary to a company pension. However, this might not necessarily be such a bonus for employees, as it's quite likely that the increased pension burden on employers will simply result in slightly lower non-pension wages (or slightly lower pay rises). In other words, it's up to employers to deal with the situation and they could do this simply by reshuffling the way that they pay you, rather than increasing the total amount they pay you.

Stakeholder pensions will basically be a form of defined contribution personal pension. What makes them attractive is the proposed transparent and low-charging structure. Charges will be limited to 1 per cent per annum and that's it. There can be no front-end loading, no initial charges and no anything else. This will make them much cheaper than most existing pensions, except the index trackers, and the chances are, surprise, surprise, that almost all stakeholder pensions will be index trackers. Still, you'll know us well enough by now to know that we think that's a good thing.

If you are already paying into a final salary company pension scheme and earn more than £30,000 pa, you won't be allowed to take out a stakeholder for yourself. But you can for someone else, such as a non-earning partner, or child. In fact, people who aren't earning can still contribute up to £3,600 to a stakeholder per year, irrespective of their age, and the government will still chip in the basic rate tax even if they're a non-taxpayer. There is concern in some quarters, then, that one of the main uses of stakeholder pensions will be tax avoidance by the very rich, who can contribute to them on behalf of non-earning spouses and children.

SIPPs

SIPP stands for self-invested personal pensions. As the name suggests, they're a form of personal pension that enable you to make the investment decisions for yourself. You have to have a scheme administrator and historically they have charged you heftily for the pleasure. This meant that you needed a fairly big fund (at least £50,000 and probably more like £100,000) to make it worthwhile. The first of the discount operators has hit the scene now, however, in the form of SippDeal (**www.sipp deal.co.uk**). They offer an extremely low-cost way of managing your own SIPP, delivering value to all, along with the possibility of a SIPP for people with smaller funds. Others will follow, including the big banks, but all credit to the trailblazer.

The flexibility they offer in payments make SIPPs particularly attractive to the self-employed. One bad year might mean the individual would prefer to make a smaller, or even no, contribution that year. He, or she, can do that without penalty. Similarly, if they enjoy a good year they can make a larger contribution, subject of course to the rules on age and percentage of earnings.

Reprise: 'You've got to have a pension, haven't you?'

We feel a little more able to answer this now and the answer is 'Nope'. While it's probably a good idea to contribute to your occupational scheme – as long as you don't switch jobs too often – in our opinion personal pension plans and AVCs are overrated. Their exorbitant charges, inflexibility and the compulsion they bring to purchase an annuity counterbalance the undoubted advantage of the tax relief they attract on contributions.

Bear in mind, though, that other investment wrappers provide tax relief, too: most importantly, the ISAs that we looked at in Chapter 3. With a pension, you get tax relief on the money you put in, but you get taxed fully on your eventual income when you retire. With an ISA, on the other hand, you don't get any tax relief on your contributions, but the eventual income comes to you free of tax. All things being equal, this amounts to the same thing. This is because we're talking about a mathematical operation called multiplication, in which it makes no difference when you do it. For example, look at the position for a higher rate taxpayer (i.e. 40 per cent) who has £1,000 to invest pre-tax and gets 9 per cent growth for three years before drawing income at a rate of 5 per cent. Tax of 40 per cent before the money goes into the ISA leaves him with £600 ('1,000 x 0.6'). This grows at 9 per cent a year for three years (that's the '1.09' in the equation) and is then drawn at a rate of 5 per cent (that's the '0.05'):

ISA: £1,000 x 0.6 x 1.09 x 1.09 x 1.09 x 0.05 = £38.85

Meanwhile, in the pension, all the money goes in up front (i.e. there's total tax relief on it), but the income gets taxed at the end:

Pension: £1,000 x 1.09 x 1.09 x 1.09 x 0.05 x 0.6 = £38.85

Each year's income is the same, for the ISA and the pension: £38.85. Not a lot of people realize this. But now you do.

Unfortunately, this position is confused by a couple of factors. First of all, the tax benefits of an ISA are not quite this simple. Although the interest on bonds and cash attracts full tax relief, there is only partial relief on the income from shares, which you get in the form of dividends. In effect, because the company that you invest in pays tax on its earnings, the income from shares is automatically taxed at the basic rate (give or take a little) – even in an ISA. You therefore only really get a tax benefit on the income from shares in an ISA if you are a higher rate taxpayer in retirement (because you avoid having to pay an extra bit). Since part of the point of going along the ISA route is to keep money in shares after retirement, this reduces their appeal somewhat, but at least you're not compelled to buy the underperforming annuity as you are with a pension. Secondly, the above example assumes that you will pay the same rate of tax in retirement as you do during your working life. In practice, your income (and therefore tax rate) in retirement is likely to be lower. Again, this might make a pension seem more attractive, but again, you're still faced with having to buy an annuity.

Other benefits of saving via the pensions route are that, if you lost your job, you'd have to use up most of your non-pension savings before you qualified for any welfare benefits. Similarly, from April 2001, any pension that you have may be protected if you are made bankrupt. The last main benefit of pensions is that the contribution limits are much higher than for ISAs. If you are already making full ISA contributions, the tax benefits of pensions become much more obvious.

We'll say more about why we don't like annuities in Chapter 5. For now we're just trying to bring all the pros and cons of defined contribution pensions together in one place. From where we're standing it looks something like this. We start off being suspicious about defined contribution pensions for the reasons that we've given. However, their appeal might be improved if the following applied:

- If the government abolished the requirement to use your fund to buy an annuity;
- If your employer contributes to your pension;
- If you expect to have a low tax rate (that is, a low income) in retirement;
- If you are a higher rate taxpayer during your working life;
- If the pension fund has low charges.

On top of these, though, there is, one overriding reason why you might want to contribute to a pension plan and that is if it's the only way you can keep your grubby paws off the money. Most other types of investment will allow you to raid your funds before you really need them, before you really should. With a pension plan, you can't get any benefit from the money until retirement, no ifs, ands or buts, and even then, apart perhaps from a lump sum, you can only use the money to provide you with an income. Be honest with yourself and if you haven't got the discipline to leave your savings untouched, then start looking around for some halfway decent pension provision: an index tracker-based PPP or AVC, a stakeholder pension or a cheap SIPP is probably going to be your best bet. Alternatively, just resolve to sit on your hands for the intervening time, as good a solution as any.

Pension resources

The Inland Revenue has all kinds of useful information available directly from your tax office or else online at **www.inlandrevenue.gov.uk**. They also have a pensions telephone helpline, which you'll find lower down.

The Inland Revenue publishes a range of pensions

booklets which are listed on the Internet at **www.inlandrevenue.gov.uk/pso/psoc.htm**. The booklets cover occupational and personal pensions and the writing is surprisingly clear and concise. You can find out about occupational schemes in the booklet PS01 and personal in PS02. If you're not happy about things, then A01 tells you how to complain! To be fair to the Inland Revenue (someone has to be sometimes), they do an excellent job these days of explaining complex situations.

The Pension Schemes Office of the Inland Revenue also has a Customer Help Desk at:

Yorke House
PO Box 62
Castle Meadow Road
Nottingham
NG2 1BG

Tel: 0115-974 1600 - for occupational pension scheme enquiries

Tel: 0115-974 1777 - for personal pension scheme and FSAVC enquiries

These lines are open to the public from 10 am to 4 pm, Monday to Friday.

The Department of Social Security also has some simple information on pensions, including the state pension and SERPS, at **www.gogetpensions.gov.uk**.

This is the place you need to go for information about the Minimum Income Guarantee: **www.dss.gov.uk/mig/002.htm**. Or phone 0800 028 11 11.

If you have a query about your occupational pension, the people you need to talk to are the Occupational Pensions Advisory Service: OPAS, 11 Belgrave Road, London SW1V 1RB. The telephone helpline is on 020 7233 8080 and there is a useful website at **www.opas.org.uk.**

Chapter 5
Annuities: Serious Business

An annuity is a very serious business.
Jane Austen, *Sense and Sensibility*

Annuities are a little bit easier to get your head round than pensions, partly because they come in fewer flavours. Even so most people wouldn't know one if they fell over it. However, despite not being the most scintillating subject in the world, you need to know and understand about annuities, you really do.

Why do you need to know about annuities?

If you are paying into a defined contribution pension, whether occupational or personal, you need to understand how best to maximize your annuity income when the time comes to take it. If you are considering whether to take out a defined contribution pension, understanding annuities could well influence your decision. If you are already drawing annuity income, it's probably also worth understanding the basis on which that income comes to you. These three groups probably account for just about everybody, so buckle down and read on.

What is an annuity?

An annuity is a stream of income payable for a defined period of time or, more usually, until death. Let's just pause here and make sure we have digested that. An annuity stops when you do. If you buy an annuity for, say, £100,000 at age 65 to give an annual income of £8,000, but you pop your clogs the next year, then the rest of the money stays with the insurance company. Your estate, and heirs, will not see one penny of it. Of course it works the other way too. Should you continue to live to a ripe old age of 110, for example, your insurance company has to keep paying out that income to you every year.

This inability to pass money on to future generations is a major drawback to annuities. However, although it is a drawback, it should not blind us to the benefit of having a guaranteed income for the rest of our natural days, and while it may not be the greatest income, it is essentially hassle-free. Some people say that annuities are risk-free, but that ignores the risk that most annuities will not grow in line with inflation and therefore your income will wither in real terms. If they do track inflation, then they'll start you off with a lower income to make up and, in any event, they won't keep up with the average earnings of society; so, over the long term, you'll still get left behind.

Normally an annuity is purchased with the funds built up in a personal pension, but the tax-free element of the pension stops there. Income from an annuity is taxable, so although you may have received the tax back on your pension contributions all those years ago, the taxman eventually gets his cut after all. As we mentioned in the last chapter, the substantial tax benefits of personal pensions come in the fact that a higher-rate taxpayer before retirement may well not be a higher-rate taxpayer after retirement. This means that having had tax relief at the higher rate, you only then pay lower rate tax on the annuity income.

An annuity is just like any other financial product, in that it can be purchased from a variety of financial institutions; it doesn't have to be bought from the manager running the pension fund. Like everything else, it pays to shop around for better rates, even though only about 30 per cent of newly retired people do so. The main factors governing how much an annuity will pay out are the annuity rate (which is pretty low these days) and your life expectancy at the time you take it out.

The annuity rate is very much a part of the problem. Its level is determined by long-term interest rates which, in turn, are defined by the yield on long-dated gilts. Huh…long-dated gilts? You remember them, from Chapter 2. They're the things which are a good place to store your money over the short-term, but which tend to be a lousy investment over the long term.

Annuities were all very well when retirements were a relatively short-lived affair (excuse the pun), but nowadays we're all living a fair bit longer. Long enough, in fact, to get us comfortably into the sorts of time periods where equities tent to provide very much better investment returns, and to provide them just as predictably.

Staying with life expectancy for a moment, in many ways it makes sense to defer buying an annuity for as long as possible, since then you get a better rate (because you won't live as long). There is of course a trade-off though, because every year without the annuity income is a year's cash foregone. Nonetheless, since gilts and therefore annuities are more suited to short investment horizons, it is generally best to leave it as late as possible. As you're starting to realize, nothing is simple when it comes to annuities. Another quirk is that women get lower annuities because they are likely to live longer. They end up with a similar amount of money, of course; it is just spread over more years.

Getting an annuity

OK, so we have built up a substantial pension from our long-term savings and now we have to buy an annuity. What?! You don't want to? Well, I'm afraid that under current legislation you have to, although you do have the flexibility of doing so any time after you retire, from the youngest retirement age of 50 up to the age of 75. There are ways of easing the transition into buying annuities and we will discuss those later. They rejoice in names like phased retirement and income drawdown schemes.

For now, let's take a look at the different flavours of annuity.

Different flavours of annuity: there are no free lunches

There's something about annuities that always makes you feel as if you're paying heftily for whatever option you choose – as if you're caught up in a system whose watchword is stinginess. It always feels as if you're not getting a very good deal. Perhaps the simple explanation is that, since the returns are linked to a poor long-term investment (that is, gilts), you're *not* actually getting a very good deal.

The important thing to remember is that you're buying an annuity with a fixed amount of money. You cannot get back any more than you put in. So all that different types of annuities do is give you your money back in different ways. If you want it inflation-proofed, it means you get less to start with. If you want your spouse to continue getting it after you die, then you get less while you are alive. To make a very simple analogy, an orange is still just one orange if it is cut into halves or quarters.

With that little preamble fixed in our head, let us look at some of the options.

First, there are 'level' annuities that pay out exactly the same amount each year until the pensioner dies. For example, a lump sum of £100,000 might pay a man of 65 £9,280 per year for the rest of his life at current annuity rates. As women generally live longer than men do, a woman of 65 would only get £7,850 per year; a woman of 60 would only get £7,100 per year. These are nice and simple.

Then there are 'level guaranteed' annuities. These pay out each year for at least five years, even if the pensioner dies in the meantime. In this case the annual payment is slightly less; the 65-year-old man would get £9,100 per year.

Next are 'joint life/last survivor' annuities, which pay a couple the same amounts each year until the second partner dies. A man of 65 and a woman of 60 would get £6,700 per year, or £7,350 if they accept a one-third reduction on the death of the male partner. Joint annuities always pay out smaller amounts than single-life annuities since they're bound to last at least as long.

Next on the list are 'inflation-linked' annuities,

which increase the annual payments by 3 or 5 per cent to give the pensioner some protection against inflation. However, they are expensive. To give you some idea of how much extra it costs to secure a 5 per cent inflation increase, the income received by a 60-year-old man from an inflation-linked annuity is initially about 40 per cent less than it is from a level one.

A different way of protecting against inflation is via so-called 'with-profits' annuities. In these, the pension fund is invested in a with-profits fund, so that annual bonuses are generated that will allow the annuity payment to grow. A similar logic applies to 'unitized' annuities where the fund is invested in unit trusts. Both these types offer the pensioner some protection against inflation because they are allowing the fund to benefit from rises in share prices. Again, though, you'll pay the price.

The strange thing is that even though the purchaser doesn't get a very good deal, selling annuities is not even a particularly profitable business to be in, and the annuity business is going through a period of very major change as a result. Some annuity providers are pulling out of the business, particularly of the standard, level business, because it doesn't pay. Against this, there has been an increase in the number of providers of so-called special rates annuities, which are more profitable. These are sold to smokers or people with health problems who have higher mortality rates.

Another type of annuity that offers higher rates are 'socio-geo-economic' annuities. These products are aimed at former manual workers and/or residents of certain parts of the UK. In other words, and let's be blunt about this, if you're a retired Geordie shipyard worker who enjoys a bottle or two of Newcastle Brown and a packet of Capstan Full Strength each day, annuity sellers will beat a path to your door.

Income drawdown

We mentioned earlier that there are ways of delaying, and phasing in, the purchase of annuities. Income drawdown and phased retirement schemes, which we'll come to in a bit, enable you to do this. We'll take a skim through the basic principles of them here.

Income drawdown enables you to delay the purchase of your annuity beyond the age of 65. In fact, you can delay taking the annuity until you are 75. It's available in personal pensions and some defined contribution occupational schemes.

As we have seen, the big problem with annuities is that their returns are essentially linked to gilts, which are a poor investment for long periods of time. As a result, delaying the purchase of your annuity is very attractive. It enables you to maintain an exposure to equities for longer and, when you eventually buy the annuity, it is for a shorter period of time (and therefore more appropriate). Also, if you die before purchasing the annuity, your pension fund passes to your heirs rather than staying with the insurance company. On top of all this, drawdown enables you to take money out of your pension fund, so that you end up having to use less to buy your annuity.

The way it works is that from when you start to take your pension benefits (between 50 and 65) until you take the annuity, you take an income from your pension fund of between 35 per cent and 100 per cent of what you would have got from a typical annuity had you taken one (the figures are set by the Government

Actuaries Department). This amount can be varied from year to year.

Essentially, the Foolish thing to do is to take the full 100 per cent drawdown and delay the purchase of the annuity for as long as possible. This is quite controversial, though. Most financial advisers will tell you that there is great risk in doing this and you must be careful to purchase your annuity when annuity rates are 'favourable'. That all sounds well and good, but the fact is that no one knows when annuity rates are favourable.

More than that, there tends to be an inverse relationship between asset prices and gilt yields (and therefore annuity rates). Broadly speaking, if the yield on an investment halves, but the income it produces stays the same, the investment has to double in price. If yields double, but the income remains the same, then the price of the investment will halve. So, if annuity rates go up, apparently enabling a greater retirement income, the chances are high that asset prices will have fallen and you'll have a smaller fund with which to buy the annuity. Similarly, if annuity rates go down, apparently giving you a smaller retirement income, then the chances are that asset prices will have risen, so you'd have a bigger pot to use to buy the annuity. To put it another way, the income that an asset can generate is generally a lot more stable than the price of that asset. So long as you keep the asset, it should be able to provide you with the same (or rather steadily growing) income.

It doesn't always work like this. Recent history in Japan has seen the equivalent of falling annuity rates combined with falling asset prices. This is unusual, but it is hard to say how unusual. Anyway, we'd say that the potential benefits of income drawdown are well worth the risks.

While we're on the subject – Equitable Life

We can illustrate this relationship between the yields and the values of assets by taking a quick look at the recent saga of Equitable Life. Essentially, the reason they've come a cropper is that they didn't understand this relationship when they offered people 'Guaranteed Annuity Contracts' back in the 1970s and '80s. In essence, they said, 'You'll get the growth that we can get in our with-profits fund and then, when the time comes, we'll guarantee a floor to the annuity rate that we'll pay you.' Sounds pretty good, doesn't it? Not surprisingly, as something of a one-way bet, they were pretty popular.

The trouble is that the annuity rates that were guaranteed back then were of the order of 12 per cent. Now, annuity rates are down to, say, 6 per cent. However, the result has been an extra-strong performance in the underlying investments. So, the holders of guaranteed annuities are getting the investment benefit of falling gilt yields, but are taking an income as if the yields hadn't fallen at all. Who has to pay for this? Well, I'm afraid it's the people in the fund who didn't have guaranteed annuities. Part of their good investment performance has to be used to pay the holders of the guaranteed annuities, but they still only get today's annuity rate of 6 per cent.

Does that sound fair? Well, not really, but then the guaranteed annuity holders did have guarantees. In the end, even the judges had a hard time agreeing on who should get what. We would say that all this is a very bad advertisement for 'with-profits' funds in general. People are entitled to a bit more certainty in their retirement planning. They really can't be expected to check every policy written by the fund that they invest in to see if they'll have to subsidize some seemingly obscure guarantee in future. The answer is to make sure that the investment returns that you get have your name firmly attached to them from the start, and that no one can take them away from you. That essentially means avoiding 'with-profits' funds

Phased retirement

Phased retirement is not to be confused with income drawdown, although the effects aren't entirely dissimilar. If you have a pension scheme that allows for 'segmentation', then it means that your scheme is, in fact, lots of little schemes rolled into one. Each small bit of the scheme is its own discrete pension, and you can take the benefits from each of them when you like, between the ages of 50 and 65. So you could, perhaps, take one bit of your pension every month from the age of 55 to 60. That way you gradually phase in your retirement benefits.

Phased retirement can be used in conjunction with income drawdown and is particularly useful for the self-employed or, indeed, anyone who wishes to wind down their workload (and income) gradually over several years. As ever, though, watch out for the costs associated with taking this type of option.

Consolidation

The disjointed and varied working lives of so many people these days mean that an individual may have a number of different pension plans. It should be possible to consolidate these into one annuity, although mixing defined benefit and defined contribution plans may not be feasible. This is probably one time when it would make sense to talk to a specialist annuity salesman, because it could substantially reduce management costs. One large fund is likely to be much more efficient than several small ones.

The Future

There is a strong, and growing, campaign to abolish the legal requirement to buy an annuity by the age of 75, or indeed to have to buy one at all with your pension fund money, a campaign we strongly support. In part, this is driven by the cohort of pensioners who have taken advantage of income drawdown plans in the last five years and can see the age limit rapidly approaching. Most likely the government will adopt a policy of gradual change rather than complete abolition. The noises that have come out so far suggest that the age of compulsory purchase may be moved back five years to 80, but implementation of the change may be delayed for several years. The other possibility is to do what the Irish have done and insist on a minimum purchase, which is at quite a low level. In their case it has been set at 50,000 Irish pounds. That does at least provide the pensioner with a very basic income in retirement, and gives him or her discretion over the remainder. At the Fool, we wholeheartedly support this campaign to abolish compulsory annuity purchase and would urge you to do so too. At the time of writing you'll find a website devoted to the issue at **www.cappa.org.uk**. This is the website of the Compulsory Annuity Purchase Protest Alliance, dedicated to scrapping the compulsory purchase requirement.

Annuities are like poker

The annuity business can perhaps be likened to a very large but serious game of poker. Although there are some fundamental drawbacks to them, principally the inability to pass on wealth to the next generation and the fact that once bought, they do not benefit from any growth, annuities do have the advantage of guaranteeing you a hassle-free income for the remainder of your life, albeit at a relatively low level.

So the poker game is a three-way match between you, your heirs and the annuity seller. If you expire early having just bought an annuity, the finance house wins hands down. If, however, you go on to cross the 100-year barrier, drawing your annuity income year after creaky old year, you are ahead and doing your little bit to beat the system. Full House to you. (Or is it Royal Flush?) Now consider the alternative scenario where, for whatever reason, you didn't buy an annuity and intend to make your heirs uncommonly wealthy. If you do die young then they get lucky. But if instead you go on living for decades more than your avaricious family expects, then your wealth will slowly be diminished by the cost of supporting your longevity (unless you have planned well for capital growth by reading Chapter 6 of this book). Indeed, without good planning it is quite possible that all your assets could be consumed in support of your lifestyle. In that case, the net result for your survivors is precisely the same as if you had bought an annuity.

Hurts your head, doesn't it?

Conclusion

After all these pros and cons, what do we think about annuities? For occupational pension holders on defined benefit schemes it isn't an issue. They get a pension from the company scheme that is determined entirely by their final salary and their length of service. Annuities do not come into their lives at all.

At the moment, those in defined contribution schemes, whether generated by personal schemes, including SIPPS, or by an occupational plan, don't have much of a choice either. They have to buy an annuity by the age of 75 as the law stands at the moment. While the law may change – and we hope it will – in the future, we have to deal with it as it stands today. On that basis, it certainly makes sense to take full advantage of being able to take 25 per cent of the pension as a tax-free lump sum and invest it separately. It also makes sense, if your circumstances allow it, to defer buying the annuity for as long as possible.

What about someone considering starting a personal pension plan that will ultimately lead to an annuity? The knowledge that the rules will probably be changed by the time the saver retires doesn't do much to help the decision-making process, because you don't know what those rules will be changed to. As ever with financial decisions, much depends on the individual's circumstances. For those without heirs, the annuity route could make some sense if their absolute priority is a hassle-free retirement. But then there's always the donkey sanctuary…

Hopefully, this chapter will have helped shed a little light on what is, in many ways, an unnecessarily complex area, and helped you to make the best of it. If you have further comments or questions to make, why not pop along to the Motley Fool's discussion board on pensions. We'd love to see you there and maybe you could even explain some of this annuity nonsense to us. We'd be insanely grateful if you would.

Anyway, to sum up on annuities, here's *Investors' Chronicle* in 1996, waxing lyrical on the insurers who sell them:

> *Insurers take their cut by investing your capital. They expect investment gains to more than pay your income. Therein lies a cautionary tale. If insurers can make more from investing your money than the income they are prepared to offer, so can you. In other words, if you don't have to buy an annuity, they are often best avoided.*

Quite.

Chapter 6
The Endlessly Replenishing Retirement Portfolio

Ye rigid ploughmen! Bear in mind
Your Labour is for future hours
Richard Henry Horne, *The Plough*

In the bulk of this book so far, we've looked at ways to build up a pot of money to provide you with an income at retirement. By and large, this falls in to a choice between pension and non-pension based savings or, quite likely, a bit of both. As we saw in Chapter 5, annuities are the vehicle for providing an income from a pension fund when you reach retirement. For your non-pension savings, though, you arrive at retirement with a pot of money, perhaps £300,000 or more, which you need to use to generate your income. How to achieve this is what we'll be looking at in this chapter.

Taking a look at your position

There you are, with your £300,000, looking at a period of (hopefully) about twenty to thirty years in which you'll need to live off it. At the moment, the money's probably in something like an index tracker, and is still growing happily every year. That sounds nice and simple: why not just cream off the amount it grows each year, leaving you with the £300,000 tucked safely in the tracker?

The answer to this is that for the purposes of generating an income, trackers aren't quite as great as when we were just leaving our savings to grow. We'll explain exactly why in a minute, but suffice to say for now that you're probably going to need to do a little bit more with your pot to make it last. And this is going to involve some new bits of information about things like shares and how they generate income. Let's start with some of the basics.

What you've been getting on your index tracker, or other investment, over the last decades has been, we hope, in the region of 6 per cent (remember that's over and above growth in average wages). This is the 'total return' − the sum total of what you've received. So far, you probably haven't had to think about what elements the total return is made up of. Well, now that we want to start drawing an income, we need to look at where the return comes from a bit more closely.

The total return is made up of the dividend and any increase in the value of the share itself. The dividend is the money paid out by companies twice a year as a kind of 'salary' to the shareholders. The increase in the value of the share is… well, that's pretty obvious really: one year a share might be worth 50p and the next year its value might have risen to 60p. Simple.

So far, so good. Now we need to apply this information to generating our income. What should you invest in? Unfortunately, there's no one clear answer to this, but we'll try to clarify some of the issues so that you can make some choices. It all boils down to the size of your pot, whether you want to keep it intact or gradually spend your capital over time, and whether you're prepared to plunge in and start buying your own individual shares.

If we cast our minds back to Chapter 2, 'How Much Do You Need?', we'll remember that, although shares do better in the long run, cash and gilts are much safer over shorter time periods. What we don't want is to have to sell any shares to provide us with spending money in the near future. If it's money we'll need to spend in the next five to ten years, then it should either come by way of income from our investments, or it should be sitting safe in a bank account somewhere, earning interest and awaiting its call-up.

The reason for this is that while the value of shares is subject to sometimes vicious ups and downs over the short term, the income that they generally pay out, in the form of dividends, is not. We'll look at this more closely in a moment – for now, just bear in mind that whenever we sell shares we increase our risk, because we might be selling them at a bad (or a good) time. So, as we've said, you should aim to cover your next five to ten years of spending needs with the income from your investments and cash sitting in a bank account.

The ideal thing is to have all of your income needs covered by the dividends that you get from a portfolio of shares. That way, you get your nice steady income and you can keep most of your money invested in shares, which, as we've seen, should give the best returns over the long term. Unfortunately, life is never that simple and, in reality, we're going to have to look beyond our dividends to provide us with spending money. The point that we're trying to make here is that the money that we're spending over the next five to ten years, to the extent that it doesn't come from our dividends, needs to be sitting safe and sound in a bank account.

Let's say that we expect to need £20,000 to spend each year and our dividends are only providing us with £15,000 of that. We should aim to have somewhere around £25,000 to £50,000 (that is, five to ten years' worth of £5,000), depending on our attitude towards risk, sitting in cash. Each year you would aim to replenish this store of cash, so that all the time you know that you can cover your next few years of spending out of income and cash. In fact, you should start this process five or ten years before retirement, gradually building up your pot of cash so that when you actually retire, you have the right balance.

How much to take?

The first thing to sort out here is what returns we expect to make on our pot of money. Remember that we expect equities to give a return relative to average earnings growth of 6 per cent a year. By the same measure, cash has a relative return of, roughly speaking, 0 per cent. So, the more of our pot we have to have in cash, the lower the returns we can expect to make. For instance, if we had £50,000 of our £300,000 in cash (that is, one sixth), then we might reduce our return expectation from 6 per cent to 5 per cent (that is, by one sixth). Not surprisingly, that would mean that we'd have less spending money, but we'd have traded some of our return for a bit more certainty.

Anyway, to keep things simple, let's assume that we have all of our pot invested in shares and that our costs are zero. We'd expect to be able to take about 6 per cent per annum from our pot to fund our retirement and we'd expect our pot (and what we can take from it) to *maintain* its value relative to what the average person is earning. If we were to take 8 per cent per year from our pot, then we'd expect our pot to be falling in relative value by 2 per cent each year. If we only take 4 per cent per year, then we should expect our pot to continue to grow at a relative rate of 2 per cent per year.

How much you take out of your retirement pot depends on your circumstances. If you've got more than enough money (apparently this is possible!) and you want to leave your non-pension savings to your children/cat's home/local bowls club, then you might even decide to keep a growing pot and take less than 6 per cent per year. However, if you don't have quite enough or don't wish to leave the money to anyone anyway, then you'll want to run down your pot gradually over time.

As you can probably imagine, though, you have to be very careful about how quickly you do this. Compound interest is working against you and, with the tables turned, it is as terrifying on the way down as it is miraculous on the way up. Let's take our annual costs of 0.5 per cent away again and assume annual returns of 5.5 per cent. If we start with a pot of £200,000 and take £16,000 from it per year (that is, 8 per cent of the starting value), then we'd expect our pot to run out after 22 years. Even if you only take a frugal-looking 6.5 per cent of your starting pot per year, just 1 per cent more than your annual returns, then you'd run out of money after 35 years. That should be enough for most retirements, but with life expectancies increasing and people retiring earlier, it could be pushing it.

You do these sums by multiplying your pot value by

your annual return each year (plus 1, so that an annual return of 5.5 per cent means multiplying by 1.055) and then deducting your withdrawal. You keep a running total of pot value and the number of years that have past. When your pot reaches zero, then you're in trouble, but you knew that, didn't you?

Bear in mind that all of this is still highly dependent on the stock market returns that are actually achieved. If it turns out that the stock market only returns 4 per cent per year (after costs and relative to earnings growth) and you're taking the 6.5 per cent that you thought was frugal, then you'd run out after 25 years. Returns of 2 per cent and a withdrawal rate of 6.5 per cent and it would all be gone after 19 years.

The best thing to do is to play with a few numbers. Put in some central case figures and see how it works out for you. Then have a look at what happens if the stock market has one of those occasional, nasty 20-year spells. How nasty they can be (or at least how nasty they've been in the past) was shown in the tables in Chapter 2, 'How Much Do You Need?' On the plus side, it's likely that, at least later on, you can allow yourself to fall behind in terms of average earnings. After all, how many 90-year-olds do you know using all the newfangled gadgets? You should still be careful, though, as there is always the possibility of things like long-term care needing to be paid for. That may indeed involve any number of specialist clever new gadgets. Certainly it would involve paying carers a wage that bears relation to the average wage.

How to take the money?

The cheapest and least risky way to take returns from shares is to take their dividend income. Not only does it avoid costs but, as we've seen, it tends to be very stable, certainly compared to the ups and downs that you can get in share prices. Companies don't like having to reduce their dividends. In fact, they like to stay within themselves, so that they have the wherewithal to make the dividends grow steadily over the years. Because of this, if you invest in a range of companies, then you're very unlikely to see your dividend income fall. If you did, then there would most likely be a fundamental problem with the economy and other investments like cash would probably be doing very badly as well (if that makes you feel any better).

Anyway, all this applies to the index trackers that we've talked about before. Just in the same way that a portfolio of shares pays dividends, so does an index tracker. There are, however, one or two problems with index trackers as far as drawing income is concerned. We'll look at this in a moment. For the time being, we need to explore this business of dividends in a bit more detail.

As far as dividends are concerned, shares come in all shapes and sizes. The 'dividend yield' of a share is the amount of income that it pays out each year, divided by its share price. That means if you invest £10,000 in a company with a dividend yield of 5 per cent, then it will provide you with an income, to start with, of £500 per year. Under current tax rules, if you're a basic-rate taxpayer, or the shares are in an ISA, then there is no further tax to pay. For shares outside of an ISA, on the other hand, higher-rate taxpayers have to make up the tax, from the 20 per cent that they're deemed to have paid already to their 40 per cent tax rate.

Some shares have 'dividend yields' of 10 per cent, some have dividend yields of 6 per cent, some have dividend yields of 3 per cent and some pay no dividends at all. Let's assume, for a moment, that we have what people call an 'efficient market'. Let's also say that we get our annual return of 6 per cent (before costs and relative to average earnings). On that basis, we'd expect a share with a dividend yield of 4 per cent to increase that dividend (relative to average earnings growth) by about 2 per cent per year. With the dividend increasing at 2 per cent per year, then the share price would have to grow at 2 per cent per year to keep the dividend yield at 4 per cent. So our total return is 4 per cent plus 2 per cent, giving 6 per cent. In the same way, we'd expect a share with a yield of 6 per cent to have a dividend which rises in line with average earnings growth, but no more and no less. Dividend yields are listed on the share pages of most broadsheet newspapers.

A share with a dividend yield higher than 6 per cent should not be able to increase it as quickly as average earnings. As a result, it is often the case that companies with dividend yields of more than this are, in fact, expected to reduce their dividend to shareholders so that they have more money to invest back into their business and can start to increase it at a decent rate again. So beware of companies with dividend yields of more than 6 per cent. The reason why the shares are that cheap relative to last year's dividend is that the stock market has most likely spotted that a reduction is on the cards.

With all this in mind, let's look again at how we might go about producing our income.

If you don't want to pick your own shares

Index trackers

If you don't want to pick your own shares, for whatever reason, then the answer for your non-pensions savings in retirement is likely to be some form of collective investment fund. It'll come as no surprise that the first type of these that we want to talk about is the good old index tracker. You might, though, be surprised to hear that for the purposes of generating an income, we don't consider them with the same almost unmitigated joy that we did when we were growing our savings.

You see, the problem with index trackers is that by definition, they have the average dividend yield of the overall stock market, less their costs. The average yield of the market is a little over 2 per cent at the time of writing so, after we've taken our 0.5 per cent away to account for charges, we're left with only about 1.5 per cent. The rest of your expected total returns would have to come from the long-term growth in the value of your tracker. So you'd have to get the other few per cent of your annual retirement income by selling a few per cent of the fund each year. As we've seen earlier, this means that you should have five to ten years' worth of this extra few per cent tucked away safely in a bank account.

Index trackers, then, can provide us with some sort of answer to our retirement income needs. They still have the advantage of low costs and of delivering the stock market's average performance but, since much of our retirement income comes from selling part of the index tracker each year, we need to have several (that is around five to ten) years' worth of this selling squirrelled away in the form of cash. So, it's low cost, but our expected long-term return would go down because of the portion of our investments that we have to keep in cash.

Higher yielding funds

The other possible candidate for a 'collective fund' solution to our retirement income needs is some form of higher yielding investment fund. This would have the advantage, compared to the index tracker, of needing less savings to be sitting in underperforming cash. However, it would have the disadvantage of reducing our expected return because of the almost certainly higher costs, and you couldn't be confident that it would produce the average return of the stock market.

What we're really looking for is a cheap high-yield equity fund, and the cheapest will almost certainly be a large investment trust. Unlike unit trusts, investment trusts are actually structured as companies. This means that, as they grow larger, they have to pass on to shareholders the benefits of 'economies of scale' in the costs of managing them. The larger investment trusts can therefore have surprisingly low charging structures. Certainly much lower than the typical unit trust, and in some cases even as low as index trackers. Investment trusts are especially suitable in retirement, since you are investing a lump sum (this negates one of the few benefits of unit trusts – that they are structured to accept regular savings).

High-yielding investment trusts are split into the UK Growth & Income sector and the UK High Income sector. As the name suggests, the latter has the highest yields (and therefore offers lower capital growth). If you want more information about investment trusts, plenty is provided by The Association of Investment Trust Companies (AITC). You can telephone them on 020 7282 5555 and, if you ask them nicely, they will send you their monthly information service which lists all the different investment trusts. There is also a great deal of information about investment trusts on the AITC's website at **www.aitc.co.uk** and on the Trustnet website at **www.trustnet.co.uk**. Of course, you could also come and talk about them with others on the dedicated discussion board on our website.

Remember that if you're not buying an index tracker, you can't be confident of the fund producing the market average (before costs). The best thing to do, therefore, is to spread your investments over several different investment trusts with the right sort of overall yield. If you spread your money between three or four investment trusts, your long-term returns (before costs) would be very unlikely to depart much from the market's average. As we've said, the most important thing is to find investment trusts with low charges and this will generally mean the larger ones.

If you're happy to hold your own shares (we promise it's not too hard)

The alternative to collective funds is the good old DIY approach. The beauty of this is that you can hand-pick the shares that go into your portfolio so that they have just the sort of dividend yield that your looking for. That way, you can minimize your costs, but also avoid keeping stacks of your money sitting around in cash. 'Ahh...,' you say, 'but how do *I* know which shares to buy?' Well it probably sounds a little scary, but really it's not so bad.

If you buy one share with a dividend yield of 4 per cent, then that's because the market reckons that it should grow at about 2 per cent per year (on top of average earnings growth, blah, blah, etc, etc). If you buy a share with a yield of 5 per cent, then the market expects relative growth of 1 per cent. Now the market certainly doesn't get it right all the time, that would be boring, but it's been doing it for a long time and it's got pretty good at it. If you put together a portfolio of 15 or so shares (and some would say fewer), in good solid British businesses across a range of different types of business, then things become fairly predictable. Assuming that your overall dividend yield starts at less than 6 per cent, then it's very unlikely that your income will fail to keep pace with average earnings growth.

Once you've bought the shares, you can just leave them to do their job. There's no need for any buying or selling, unless you want to try to be clever, but trying to be clever usually doesn't get you very far. By leaving the shares untouched, you minimize your costs and maximize your returns. The only real time to think about selling shares is when one of your shares has done a bit too well and the *income* from it makes up too large a proportion of your total *income* (more than about 20 per cent would be uncomfortable). In this case it might be worth selling a little of it and buying a bit more of another holding, or something else entirely.

In short, it is a fairly straightforward matter, if approached with good common sense, to construct a portfolio of shares that gives you the income you'll need in retirement with very little hassle. We came up with this list in December 2000:

Company	Dividend yield (%)		
	Last Year	This Year*	Next Year*
United Utilities	6.9	7.1	7.3
ICI	6.2	6.2	3.4
Powergen	6.1	6.4	6.6
Scottish & Newcastle	5.8	6.2	6.7
Scottish Power	5.0	5.3	5.5
BAT	5.2	5.6	6.1
Lattice	4.9	4.9	5.0
Invensys	5.0	5.1	5.4
Marks & Spencer	4.8	4.8	4.9
Bass	4.6	4.8	5.0
Royal & Sun Alliance	4.6	4.9	5.2
Imperial Tobacco	4.5	4.8	5.2
Alliance & Leicester	4.4	4.9	5.4
British Airways	4.5	4.5	4.5
Scot. & S'thern E'gy	4.4	4.7	5.0
Boots	4.2	4.4	4.6
Hilton	4.1	4.5	4.8
Gt. Universal Stores	4.1	4.1	4.3
Portfolio Yield (%)	5.0	5.2	5.3
% Annual Increase		4.4	1.8

*Based on analysts' forecasts

The 18 shares in the list are all the shares we could find with total market values in the top 100 in the country and yields, based on last year's dividend, of at least 4 per cent. If we bought equal pound amounts of these shares, we'd have had a yield of 5 per cent from them last year. Enough for a £20,000 income off £400,000. That income would be increasing to £20,800 this year (based on analysts' forecasts). However, next year we'd be increasing only by 1.8 per cent to £21,200 because of an expected dividend cut from ICI. Still, at least we'd still be going upwards and the dividend cut should enable ICI to grow its reduced dividend more rapidly in future.

So, where does all this leave us?

Since buying and selling shares involves costs and adds to risk, you should aim to fund your retirement from income paid out by your investments. If you do need to spend some of your investment capital, aim to have it in a low-risk investment, probably cash, about five or ten years or more before you need to spend it.

Assuming that you are aiming for a retirement of 25 years or more, you can take surprisingly little from your pot of money over the years without it running out. On the whole, if you're able to, it's probably best to take only your expected investment returns, or less, in the form of income.

Finally, the most effective way to provide your retirement income from non-pension savings is a diversified portfolio of higher-yielding shares. If you really don't want to bother buying your own shares, then you'll have to choose between using an index tracker and keeping a relatively large proportion of your savings in cash, or using several cheap and higher-yielding investment trusts. The latter option will clearly involve a bit more research.

Chapter 7
So You Want To Retire Early?

Term, holidays, term, holidays, till we leave school,
and then work, work, work till we die.
C.S. Lewis

Walks in the park. Lazy mornings chatting around the kitchen table, a pot of freshly brewed coffee steaming gently in front of you. Time, above all, time...

Yes, if all this talk of retirement has made you think that you might like to join this elite group as soon as possible, then this chapter is for you. Retiring early is the dream of many of us and indeed the concept of a specific 'retirement age' is as obsolete these days as the idea that most of us will stay in a single job for the entire span of our working lives. Actually, even talking about the notion of 'retiring' is too simplistic. Instead of a final retirement, many people, especially those taking 'early' retirement, will move to part-time working, choosing as and when they wish to work and only taking on assignments that they feel inspired by and feel motivated to carry out.

Looking at the question of early retirement in this way gives us a lot of flexibility when we look at our financial requirements, particularly when we reckon that the lifestyle of the 'semi-retired' person, or the 'downshifter', may be a lot less expensive. It doesn't cost much to live in west Wales, and even just moving out of commuting distance from a major city can push your expenses down dramatically.

Many people think that the basic requirement for retiring early is simple: money. That's true, but even more than this, retiring early is an attitude of mind. If you carry on working you will certainly accumulate more money, yet for some people however much money they have is never enough. The essence of retiring early is to be able to say: 'I have enough.' This means doing some serious thinking about just what your life goals are, why you value them and how much you value them. Once you've figured out what it is you really want to do when you've retired early, you'll be able to start mapping out a path towards it. If you are content to live in a smaller house outside London, rather than a four-bedroom house in Fulham, you probably have the right mental attitude to seriously consider retiring early (and, if you own that house in Fulham outright, you probably have the money too!).

Anyway, enough of that. The two main elements of a plan to retire early are the need to accumulate our pot of money sooner, and the need to make it last longer. In typical Foolish fashion, let's start with the second of these.

Making it last

If we retire early, then we naturally expect to be retired for longer. Indeed, that's exactly why we're doing it. So this means that our savings have got to last us longer. We've seen in Chapter 6, 'The Endlessly Replenishing

Retirement Portfolio', that the longer our retirement, the lower our 'withdrawal rate' can be. In fact, as we look at retirements lasting 30 years or more, we find that our withdrawal rate from our non-pension savings can be barely more than the return we expect to get from our investments (over and above growth in average earnings).

The same applies to the income from any pensions that we might have. With defined benefit pensions, retiring early means that we'll have fewer years and a lower leaving salary from which to work out our pension benefits. With defined contribution benefits, on the other hand, the annuities that we have to buy give a lower income if we buy them sooner, since the insurance company expects to have to pay you for longer.

In fact, while we're on the subject of annuities, it's worth remembering that they become less and less attractive as your retirement gets longer because the gilts, on which their returns are based, are a bad long-term investment (have we mentioned this before?). So, the earlier you want to retire, the less you should focus on pensions to provide you with your retirement income, and the more you should focus on a portfolio of high-yielding shares.

If that's beginning to sound a little scary, then that's perhaps because it is. We'll make no bones about it. Leaving yourself with a long time to live without earning money is not going to be achieved without effort. You'll have heard people say, 'You can't have your cake and eat it.' We've no idea at all why they say this; the whole point of having a cake is to eat it. Instead, we'll say that you can't make an omelette without breaking eggs. But then who cares about breaking a few eggs? Anyway, we hope you get the picture. To secure an early (and well-funded) retirement, you've got to try to tweak everything in your favour and that might take some effort on your part. For instance, it's no time to be squeamish about generating your retirement income from a portfolio of high-yielding shares as discussed in Chapter 6. If you can save yourself 0.5 per cent per year in costs by doing it this way, as opposed to using an investment fund, then that's 0.5 per cent per year that's going to make a big difference to your retirement income (and, of course, to how soon you can retire). It's also no time for having a large pile of cash sitting around 'just in case'. You need the extra return that your money is likely to be earning from being invested in shares.

Even so, no matter how much you tweak things in your favour, leaving yourself a long retirement is likely to mean that, for the same level of retirement income, you're going to need a bigger pot of savings and you're going to need it sooner. Sheeshh… This isn't getting any easier.

Enough is enough

OK, so we need a big pot of money and we need it quick! There are two ways to look at this. First of all, let's have another look at the size of our pot. When we looked at making it last, we concluded that we'd need more than otherwise *for the same level of retirement income*. The answer is, of course, that we don't expect the same level of retirement income. Hey, the whole point of this is that we reach a level where we say, 'That's it, I've got enough!' The first way to make that easier is to lower your expectations of what's enough.

There's no way we can really help you with this,

other than to say go back to Chapter 2, in particular
SarcoramphusPapa's excellent post and have another go
at deciding what really is and what really isn't an expensive luxury. You'll reach the magic point an awful lot
sooner if, for instance, you settle for running a ten-year-
old Lada instead of a brand new Mercedes.

Economizing doesn't just start with retirement either.
Running that Lada throughout your working life will
mean you can save that much more and, as we'll see
when we get there (all in good time), saving more, especially early on, is what retiring early is all about. The idea
of 'maintaining your standard of living' in retirement is
just as relevant when you retire early. There's no point
living until 45 with a Mercedes on the driveway and
then saying, 'There… that's it, I'm done with flash cars
now. Honey, where's my hair shirt?' It won't work.
Similarly, if you're happy with a Lada in your early years,
why keep saving so that you've got enough to drive
around in the Merc when you stop work? The reality is
that you should aim to lead the same sort of lifestyle
throughout your life. That way, you'll slip seamlessly
into retirement when it comes along. It's a question of
working out the best balance. Be realistic, though.
There's no point in retiring at 45 if it means that you
don't give yourself enough time to earn the money you
need to enjoy life, both before and after retirement.

Saving it up

The final part of the equation is how quickly you can
build up your pot of money. Only by considering this
can you hope to strike the right balance between saving
now and using those savings later, since it helps you

work out when you can move from the one to the other.

Saving money is all about compounding your investment returns and compounding is all about putting away as much money as possible in the first place, leaving it for a long time and getting a good rate of return. Of these, the rate of return that we can *expect* to get is perhaps the hardest thing for us to affect. Sure we can hope and try to get market-beating returns by investing in this share or that, and, indeed, much of the discussion on the Motley Fool website is about trying to do just that. The thing is, though, that the vast majority of professional fund managers fail, and it would be foolish, not Foolish, for us to *expect* to do any better. We can certainly try, but in terms of what you factor into your plans, the best you can do is consider the returns of an index tracker, and our best guess about what they might produce is the 5.5 per cent that we came up with in Chapter 2. If it turns out that you do a bit better than this, then you might be able to retire a bit sooner than planned. If it turns out that you do worse, then we're afraid that it'll be another few years of ticking boxes down at the shoe factory. Still, worse things happen at sea (apparently).

The other two factors affecting the growth in our savings – putting away as much as possible and leaving it for a long time – are very much within our control. So, if you want to retire early, then start early and save hard, Fool! But you knew that, didn't you?

Let's have a look at how these two factors affect things. Assuming that our savings grow at 5.5 per cent per year, then the following table shows the pot that we can expect to build up and the pre-tax income that we could expect to draw from it (again assuming 5.5 per cent) for various time periods.

Time period	Saving £200 per month		Saving £400 per month		Saving £600 per month		Saving £800 per month	
	Total pot	Annual income @ 5.5%	Total pot	Annual income @ 5.5%	Total pot	Annual income @ 5.5%	Total pot	Annual income @ 5.5%
10 years	£31,814	£1,750	£63,628	£3,500	£95,442	£5,249	£127,256	£6,999
15 years	£55,370	£3,045	£110,740	£6,091	£166,110	£9,136	£221,480	£12,181
20 years	£86,157	£4,739	£172,313	£9,477	£258,470	£14,216	£344,627	£18,954
25 years	£126,394	£6,952	£252,787	£13,903	£379,181	£20,855	£505,575	£27,807
30 years	£178,982	£9,844	£357,964	£19,689	£536,946	£29,532	£715,928	£39,376

The same caveats apply to this as applied to the sums we did in Chapter 3. In particular it assumes that everything, including the money you're saving, is relative to the average wage today. So, you'd have to increase the amount you're saving monthly alongside inflation and increases in average wages (at the moment they amount to about 4 to 5 per cent per year between them). We've also assumed a growth rate of 5.5 per cent. This may or may not turn out to be accurate, it's just our best guess at it (did we say that before?!).

Even so, the figures show some interesting things. For instance, we can reach our £7,000 per year crofting lifestyle in the Hebrides after about 25 years at £200 per month, but we could expect to get there after just ten years if we could stash away £800 per month. Of course, saving at that rate means that you'd probably have to put up with the equivalent of that crofting lifestyle while you're doing it (no Friday night trips to the cinema followed by the Ruby Tandoori, unfortunately). But that's just the point: we're looking to maintain a similar standard of living throughout our lives.

What about the £15,000 per year that we targeted at the beginning of the book? Well, at £200 per month, we can see that early retirement is pretty much out of the question (unless we get a helping hand from Great-Aunt Mabel or, say, Chris Tarrant along the way). At £400, we could hope to get there after just over 25 years but, at £600, we're almost there in 20 years. Quite where you and your plans fit into this picture depends on how much you earn and the balance that it enables you to strike between the cost of your lifestyle and retiring early.

All of which brings us back to what we said at the beginning of the chapter: retiring early is an attitude of mind. For most of us, it will take a fair amount of determination and some single-minded sacrifice, but if that kind of behaviour is in your nature then there are some major rewards to be reaped. Or you can be like everyone else and just keep chucking a pound at the lottery every week. It's up to you!

Chapter 8
Your House: Asset or Liability?

Saving is a very fine thing. Especially when your parents have done it for you.
Winston Churchill

Two features loom large for most of us looking at our personal balance sheet during our working lives. One is the value of our house, and the second is the size of our mortgage. But after retirement we only want the house, not the mortgage (don't know about you, but I've never much wanted the mortgage either), and this chapter will help you achieve that. While we are working our house is a place to spend weekends, watch telly in the evenings, raise the kids and entertain. The fact that it may have appreciated in value so much that it has become the repository of most of our wealth is a pleasant side effect.

Not everyone has enjoyed such a massive appreciation in values as homeowners in and around London but, for most of us, a house is still our largest single asset. The costs of running a family house can normally be easily met while we are working, and by far the biggest cost is buying it, in other words the mortgage.

Attitudes to mortgages have changed so much in the last few decades it is hard to believe that we are dealing with the same population. In the 1960s and '70s a mortgage was something that hung around your neck like a dead weight. But even getting a mortgage then was an achievement. The Bank of England kept a close eye on the amounts building societies were lending and simply restricted funds if they felt the market was getting too frothy. Sometimes, you just couldn't get a mortgage because the funds weren't available.

Banks didn't touch this market. They stuck to business and corporate lending. So house prices were pretty subdued in this environment of a restricted supply of money. There were little booms now and again as the economy had a short-lived growth spurt, but overall the '60s and '70s were a period of financial stringency and falling standards of living, at least on a comparative basis. People wanted houses but they either couldn't afford them or couldn't get the money, which more or less amounts to the same thing.

Then in 1980 there was a revolution. Geoffrey Howe, Mrs Thatcher's first Chancellor of the Exchequer, lifted a great swathe of regulations on the banking and finance sector and removed foreign exchange controls. Even though we were in the middle of a recession, the public suddenly found that they had access to funds with which to buy a house. At the same time, the government began encouraging the sale of council houses to tenants to foster the idea of becoming a nation of homeowners. Tax breaks on mortgages were very attractive. At that time, virtually all the interest could be offset against your tax bill and this combination of factors, aided by a rapidly growing economy, soon ignited a massive house-price boom. Phrases such as 'I am under-mortgaged' became prevalent, and a bit of cheap mortgage debt was almost seen as a good thing.

Even the short-lived 1987 stock market crash couldn't prevent the housing market rising to levels previously unheard of. And it wasn't until the recession at the turn of the decade that house prices came back to lower levels. But this housing collapse was different to previous ones in one major aspect. Inflation was by now no longer a major feature of the British economic landscape, so the fall in prices was visible in nominal terms, that is, in actual pounds, as well as in real, post-inflation terms. It was round then that the phrase 'negative equity', where a mortgage exceeds the value of the house, was heard for the first time. And not the last.

Should we buy our homes?

Before we get into the hows and whys of owning homes in retirement, though, there's a rather more fundamental question that needs answering. Should we be owning our home in the first place? Sure it's nice not to have a landlord telling us not to spoil his nice walls with picture hooks, but does it make financial sense? Many of our friends across the English Channel, where home ownership tends to be much lower, don't seem to think so. So who's getting it right?

Well, the Belgians might be right to devote so much of their national efforts to the fine art of chocolate making and the French might be right to drink the stuff for breakfast, but we're pretty sure the general population in France and Belgium is getting this business of home ownership wrong. It's only the general population that's missing the point, though. You see, every property has to be owned by someone, somewhere, and we're prepared to bet that those someones are doing very well, thank you, by renting these properties out. After all, if the landlords didn't find it profitable to do this, then they'd redirect their capital to something better, like that *chocolaterie* down the road. So what is it that makes property attractive as an investment?

The first thing to spot about property is that it is a *real* asset. 'Real' as in it is actually there: bricks and mortar. As a real asset, it is worth what people are prepared to pay for it. This is very similar to shares, but it is very unlike other types of investments, such as gilts and cash, which are worth a fixed amount of pounds. The value of gilts and cash (which you might call *nominal* assets) is defined by the value of the pounds that they represent. If the pound's value falls, then your nominal assets will be worth less. On the other hand, your real assets, such as shares and property, will still be worth whatever someone is prepared to pay for them. Over the long term, inflation has meant that the tendency has been for the pound's value to fall. In fact, since the economy (including the government) operates by investing a large number of borrowed pounds, there are good reasons for thinking that if the value of the pound consistently rose, we'd eventually all go bust.

Economic policy is therefore organized to allow a steady decline in the pound's value. This is clear from the Bank of England's inflation target of 2.5 per cent. The aim is not to maintain the value of the pound, but to allow it to fall steadily. Over the long term, the interest earned on cash and gilts has been scant consolation for this. The effect is that investing in real assets such as shares and property, although it introduces a certain amount of short-term risk, is the best way of maintaining or increasing the value of your capital over the long term.

The other main thing about property as an investment is that, because you generally have to buy it in a big chunk and most of us can't afford to buy these big chunks outright, we tend to have to borrow big sums of money from someone else to do it. When we borrow money to buy a house, we are borrowing a fixed (that is, nominal) sum to invest in a real asset. This is called gearing. If we buy a house for £100,000 with a £90,000 mortgage, then we have invested £10,000 ourselves. If the house then increases in value by 10 per cent to £110,000, the value of the £10,000 that we put in has actually increased by 100 per cent to £20,000 because we still only owe £90,000 on the mortgage. However, the flip side to this is that, if the value of the house falls by 10 per cent to £90,000, then the value of the £10,000 that we put in has fallen by 100 per cent, to zero. Our short-term risk is dramatically increased but, since we expect the value of our house to increase over the long term (if only because of inflation and increases in average earnings), our long-term returns should also be increased. This gearing effect is, for many, one of the attractive aspects to property as an investment.

Should we buy other people's homes?

All this is beginning to make property sound attractive as an investment, and it is, so why don't we all put our shares away and buy properties to rent out to other people? The simple answer to this is that we can't because, by definition, if we're keen to buy our own homes then there won't be enough of them to go around. Still, some people will have the money to do it, so how about it?

The problem is that property is a difficult thing to invest in. You can't just set up a standing order for £100 per month to buy a share in the 'property market average', as you can the 'stock market average' when you purchase an index tracker, since there is no such thing as a 'property exchange'. This means that the process of buying and selling property is fairly expensive, involving, amongst other things, surveys, legal fees, and extra stamp duty. There are also costs involved in managing the property once you've bought it. Letting agents will typically charge around 10 per cent to 15 per cent of the gross rent paid on the property. If you're prepared to do this bit yourself then, even if you think you can trust yourself to do it well, it will take up a lot of your time. Time which could have been spent earning money.

The real problem is that all these costs are magnified by the 'gearing' we talked about a moment ago. The costs are fixed or dependent on the total value of the property. This means that if you buy a property with a mortgage and then rent it out, a disproportionate amount of the equity that you put into it and the net rent that you receive from it, after paying the mortgage interest, will disappear in charges. If you had a mortgage on 90 per cent of a property, then you would most likely find that all of your net rental income disappeared in charges. Of course, you're hoping that the gearing effect will magnify the increase in value of your property, but that's just hope, isn't it? Traditionally, the rental income from a property makes up a large proportion of the total returns. Large capital increases over the last couple of decades have tended to wash over this, but it would be foolish, not Foolish, to expect things to carry on like that.

If you have the money to buy a property without a mortgage, then many of these problems fall away. When you arrive at retirement with your £300,000 or so, then using part of it to buy a property to let can be attractive. As we've said, the rent tends to make up a large part of the total returns and, in retirement, this could be used to your advantage. In essence, the rent could provide a steady income, which ought to increase along with average wages. The detail of which property to buy and how to go about doing it are beyond the scope of this book but, as ever, thinking long term and doing things efficiently are the keys.

A Foolish plan for a house in retirement

Anyway, after that diversion, let's return to our own homes and what to do with them or, more importantly, what to do with that mortgage. When you're growing your investments over the years up to retirement, you can argue that it's more important to build up your equity investments than to pay off your mortgage. However, when you reach retirement and are looking to generate a low-risk income, having a mortgage becomes increasingly hard to justify. After all, we're after a steady income stream, so having to pay an unsteady stream of mortgage interest isn't going to help much.

So, as the Foolish investor approaches retirement, he or she should do their best to ensure that the mortgage is paid off, or at least that there is a plan to pay it off before retirement. In fact most people have already done this. Apparently only 4 per cent of owner-occupiers over 65 had a mortgage in 1997/8, although that partly reflects the attitudes an older generation had to debt. Nowadays, paying off the mortgage appears to be less of a priority and 'interest-only' mortgages have become increasingly popular. This will result in more and more people arriving at retirement with a mortgage. Of course, if they've been proper Fools, they'll have been putting the money saved by paying only the interest into investments, and retirement is the time to use those investments to get rid of the mortgage.

It may be that it is not possible to pay off the mortgage from existing resources. In that case you should think carefully about downsizing. Sell the house, repay the mortgage and buy something with the balance. It might be a bit painful, but investing when you're still carrying debt increases your risks, and retirement is a time for keeping your risks low. The only two caveats to that are if the mortgage is going to mature very soon after retirement, or if you are expecting a large lump sum – and I mean an inheritance, not a lottery win.

So, having paid off the mortgage, we are free to decide what to do with the house. For most people, of course, a house is far more than just a roof and four walls to keep the rain off. It is a place of memories, where families have grown up with parties and all sorts of events and celebrations. Nevertheless, the house that was suitable for a growing family and people at work probably isn't the right one for a family at leisure, and a smaller one too.

For a start, the requirement to be close to work, or at least somewhere convenient to commute from, is no longer crucial. Every commuter knows that house prices decrease exponentially from tube and railway stations. If you can, why not take advantage of that: sell up and move somewhere cheaper? There is no capital gains tax payable on your main residence, so the money freed up can go straight into your pot of investments to generate more income. Buying a smaller, and cheaper, house could also take you into a lower council tax band. All these things should help your retirement income go further.

Size is another issue. The large family home for numerous children will feel decidedly empty once they have flown the nest. Naturally, they'll come to visit from time to time, probably with grandchildren too. But ask yourselves seriously whether you need to maintain a large house just for odd visits from family and friends. And don't forget big houses take more looking after than smaller ones. Whether it is just heating or the periodic repainting, those bills seem to be much larger once your income has fallen to lower levels than you were used to.

If you hadn't noticed, getting old affects you physically, too, and you might find that your mobility and balance aren't all they used to be. That flight of stairs you used to bound up and down in your thirties can be a real obstacle with stiffer limbs in your seventies and eighties. It is perfectly feasible to put in stair lifts and grab rails, but that all costs money. In addition, access to houses is not always very convenient, possibly because of steps or narrow pavements. It's a lot easier to deal with this sort of issue ahead of events.

There is no simple answer to the issue of finding the best place to live when you retire, but some things hold true wherever you are. The first of these is access to transport. While you may be able to drive at the moment, you need to face the reality that, for whatever reason, you will have to stop at some point in the future. When that happens you will be forced to rely on public transport or taxis. Ideally, you need to be somewhere close to a bus route, or perhaps a railway station. Hmm, this seems to be taking us back into the commuter belt again. Well, not necessarily, it could be in a smaller town away from the big metropolises.

Another issue to bear in mind is shops and facilities. Without regular trips to work, just getting those little extras can mean a major expedition in the car to a shopping centre. It is far more convenient if you can take a short walk and get the odd loaf of bread from the local shops. The same applies to things like chemists and doctors' surgeries. A surgery within walking distance or a short bus ride away makes life much easier than having to get in the car.

Whatever you decide to do, do it early. Remember when you were 25? You'd be down the pub on a Saturday night, all night, then get up on a Sunday and play 90 minutes of Sunday League soccer and feel just great by lunchtime. At 35, those pints of beer don't disperse quite so easily. Well, unfortunately, it's a sad fact of life that those ten-year gaps don't get any easier. Moving at 65 might seem like an exciting start to retirement, but at 75 you might not relish it quite so much. Moreover, moving early gives you more time to meet your new neighbours and integrate yourself into the local community.

Equity release schemes

One issue we need to cover for the sake of completeness is home equity release. The way this works is that you swap your house, or part of it, for an income during your lifetime. So, you get a bit of income for the rest of your life but, when you die, your house goes to the company that provided you with the income. Does that sound familiar? It should do, because it's basically very similar to an annuity, which we looked at in Chapter 5. It also suffers from the same problems as annuities, the number one problem being that the providers use very low-risk, low-return assets (basically gilts) to provide you with your income. The upshot of this is that the swap will generally be a very poor deal. It will almost invariably make more sense to sell the property and live somewhere a bit cheaper. Anyway, at least you now know it's an option, even if it's a pretty rotten one.

Residential care

At some point, generally for medical reasons, many people find they just can't cope with living on their own any more. In this case, a residential home is the answer, unless you can come to some arrangement with other members of the family. But residential care is expensive; it starts at £15,000 a year and goes up. In fact you should probably reckon to spend upwards of £20,000 a year if you need to go into a home. To put this into perspective, you would need an annuity of around £200,000, or the income from a pension pot worth £330,000 returning 6 per cent a year. If the pot is smaller than that, and you have to raid the capital, it can chew through your savings pretty rapidly.

Whichever way you look at it, residential and nursing care is expensive. Unless the resident has been fortunate enough to build up a large amount of capital, or have a big pension, the only way to fund the expense is by selling the house, or possibly using an equity release plan.

For the next generation, half-hoping to inherit granny's house, the erosion of that capital could be a galling process. And don't expect the government to bail you out. A recent Royal Commission recommended that individuals should be able to keep £60,000 worth of assets before the local authority started to pick up the tab. But the DSS, in its reply, said that anyone with assets of over £16,000 (to be increased to £18,000) would have to pay the full cost. Below that, the state will pay the medical costs but not the accommodation costs. If you're thinking of transferring the property out of your name to avoid it being sold to fund nursing care, there's a section on this in Chapter 10.

Finally, we should note that it is possible to buy insurance to cover the cost of going into a residential or nursing home. However, as you might expect, premiums are high and related to age and health. The old adage that you get 'owt' for nowt applies strongly here. As a rule of thumb, you are generally better off investing than paying insurance premiums.

Conclusion

Housing is crucial for everyone, but it assumes critical importance for older people. After a lifetime of work, the house and home becomes the centre of your life, partly because you will spend most of your time there. Ensuring it is bought and paid for before you retire is probably the most Foolish thing you can do. Once you have done that, you have the option of staying there or moving into something else that might be more suitable for retirement. In essence, owning your own home gives you more options with your retirement finances and it reduces the risks in your net retirement income.

Chapter 9
Silver Surfers of the World Unite!

Knowledge is of two kinds. We know a subject ourselves,
or we know where we can find information upon it.
Samuel Johnson

Imagine a group of people, who are knowledgeable, have savings and some spare time. Could there be a section of society better suited to the Internet than retired people? In fact so numerous are they, and such a significant group do they represent, that they have been given their own label: silver surfers. If you're retired and you haven't logged on to the Internet yet, and don't know what all the fuss is about, then this chapter is for you.

Transport can be tricky when you're older. It's expensive and can be difficult to use. So anything that reduces the need to travel is probably going to be immensely appealing to you, and the Internet does this in a very efficient way: by offering goods and services to individuals at home.

If you've never used a computer before, don't be scared. They are tools, not masters, just like a telephone. Enrol for a course at your local college or evening school and learn the basics: you won't regret it. A good, basic reference book is the *Rough Guide to the Internet*.

Here's a simple list of things the Internet can do, for starters. Then we'll go through each one to explain how to make the best of it. On the Internet you can:

- Shop
- Bank
- Communicate with friends and relatives
- Research your hobbies and sports
- Communicate with the state and ensure you get all your benefits
- Research and run your investment portfolio
- Monitor your health

Shopping is a doddle

Let's face it, fun though it might be to spend the odd afternoon browsing through a bookshop, much of the weekly shop is a grind, especially if it means a trip to the local superstore rather than the friendly corner shop. Negotiating all those aisles with an independently minded shopping trolley and contending with traffic jams of other shoppers (and their screaming kids) can be hard work. And after that, you have to lug it all to the car, assuming you can find the vehicle again in the 5,000-space car park, drive it home and then unpack it. Wouldn't it be easier if you could just find out what the special offers are, order what you need and then get someone to deliver it? Well, you can. Most of the major supermarket chains have excellent Internet shopping services.

- **www.tesco.com**. Tesco operates Tesco Direct, and is reputed to be the world's largest online grocery company. Everything you would expect to find in a Tesco store will be there, including spe-

cial promotions.
- **www.iceland.co.uk** is another major retailer with a particularly good site.

What's best of all is that they package everything up and bring it direct to your home at the time you want. Normally the service is free, although some firms do charge a delivery fee of £5 for orders under £40.

Of course it isn't only groceries that you can buy on the Internet. Below are a few other handy retailers and services.

- **www.amazon.co.uk** – perhaps the most well-known Internet retailer, or e-tailer as they are sometimes called. Not only does it sell books and CDs but a whole host of other stuff too.

However, despite all the hype, Amazon is not always the cheapest. To make sure you are getting the best deal you should check one of the shopping search engines:

- **www.shopsmart.com**;
- **www.priceoffers.co.uk**, which has an alert service to tell you when the product you want comes up on offer;
- **www.bigsave.com**, which gives you £5 off on a purchase over £10.

Computers mean we are moving towards the paperless office and home, but for those who still need these things, you'll find a cheap supplier of stationery at

- **www.staples.co.uk**.

Finally, even dealing with your phone and fax facilities can be cheaper and easier on the Internet.

- **www.axstel.com** has all sorts of special mobile phone deals;
- **www.efax.com** offers free fax services;
- **www.phonebills.org.uk** allows you to compare phone bills;
- **www.genie.co.uk** will send free SMS (short messaging system) messages to your mobile phone for news, share prices, sports results and so on.

If you really can't find what you are looking for on any of these, then you'll have to use a search engine, such as:

- **www.copernic.com**, a search engine that uses all the other search engines;
- **www.google.com**, another good search engine;
- **www.yahoo.co.uk**, which has a lot of links to online shopping sites.

As you get older, and you feel you have better things to do than brave the high street or hypermarket frenzy, this Internet shopping lark is going to get even more appealing. It really is dead good. Give it a go.

Banking is easy too

We have all read and heard about the branch closure programmes that the major banks have been trying to implement. That process is being aided and abetted by the continuing mergers in the banking sector. Early in 2000, the Royal Bank of Scotland succeeded in its bid for National Westminster, and the summer of that year saw Barclays Bank take over the Woolwich. All this is being done to cut costs. These High Street branches are on expensive property, they need a lot of security and cost a lot to staff. But while cutting smaller branches cuts costs, it can be a major blow for people who depend on them.

There's some consolation, though. In parallel with this programme of branch closures, the banks have been building up their Internet banking facilities in a big way. You can do everything with an Internet bank that you do with a 'real' bank and even more. Many people are familiar with

- **www.egg.co.uk**, the new bank from the Prudential;
- **www.if.co.uk** from the Halifax;
- **www.smile.co.uk** from the Co-op,

and many, many more. In fact it is not only the High Street UK banks that are running online banking facilities on the Internet. New competitors are entering the fray from the worlds of insurance and foreign banking. While it's true that there have been some security problems, they are small in the overall scale of things and will undoubtedly be resolved. There is little doubt that e-banking is here to stay.

Although it's not quite banking, there is also a site that compares utility bills, which may help you cut down on costs. This is at

- **www.buy.co.uk/personal/index.asp**.

E-mail is so easy

The oldies are always complaining that the younger generation never call them, but increasingly, people are becoming reluctant to phone or visit in case their target is busy, asleep, in the middle of making a soufflé or whatever. Also, making a phone call can be quite time-consuming. This is why e-mail is so much more polite and easy to use. You can send it when it suits you, and you can reply when it suits you. No more rushing up from the meal table to answer an urgently ringing phone; the e-mail arrives silently and you answer it at your discretion. And it has two other great features, too. You can attach things, like photographs; and it is very cheap. An e-mail to your nephew in Australia costs no more than the one you send to Fred around the corner to arrange a fishing trip. Once you have logged on to the Internet the additional cost of e-mail is zero.

Hobbies and sports

Almost all sports and hobbies have websites devoted to them these days, and this provides a great way of keeping in touch with all the news and gossip. Many have discussion facilities to aid this process.

Talking to the government

After a slow start, the government is providing more and more information through the Internet and has pledged that all their services will be online by 2005. Below are some of the most useful government sites and others related to similar issues.

- **www.dss.gov.uk/lifeevent/benefits/retire ment_pension_forecast.htm#elec**: go to this site for a forecast of your National Insurance pension. You can also download the form.
- **www.dss.gov.uk/index.htm** allows you to check the whole range of benefits you might be entitled to.
- **www.inlandrevenue.gov.uk** is the Inland Revenue site, which offers help with your income tax.
- **www.open.gov.uk** gives a very comprehensive overview if you really aren't sure which bit of the government you want.

The government also finances the Occupational Pensions Advisory Service at

- **www.opas.org.uk** Go there if you have a query about your occupational pension.

Not really government, but very useful nonetheless is a site we've already mentioned several times in this book – the Age Concern site at

- **www.ageconcern.co.uk**.

If you want to lobby your MP directly, there's a very useful site,

- **www.faxyourmp.co.uk**, which allows you to fax your MP via the Internet easily and free of charge. It's the kind of thing the Internet is all about: make use of it!

Research and run your investments

Of all the benefits ushered in by the Internet, it's hard to think of anything more dramatic and symptomatic than what it's done to the world of finance and investing. For example, finding out a share price used to be a slow, laborious process that usually involved scanning the next day's papers; now it's possible to get them live for a small fee, or free if you're prepared to wait 20 minutes. There are so many useful websites it's hard to know where to start, but we certainly hope that you will visit our website at

- **www.fool.co.uk**.

Here you can find the routine data of share prices, company results and lots of financial comment. But actually, we think it's the discussion boards that you'll find most useful of all: this is where members of the community post their thoughts on companies and all aspects of investing. Another Fool, Nigel Roberts, has written a book, *The Fool's Guide to Online Investing*, which goes into all this in much more detail, so I won't repeat it all here, but there are a few useful sites that I can point out in a bit.

Share prices are in many ways the least useful aspect of what the Internet offers. After all, few of us need to check the value of our house every day, and it's the same with shares. Trading shares is a small part of the Foolish investor's activities. Each time you trade you pay commission to a broker, even if it's only £10 with Internet brokers; and if you are buying shares you have to pay stamp duty of 0.5 per cent each time. Generally, the

Foolish aim is to minimize trading as much as possible; but when you do trade, an Internet broker will almost certainly give you the best deal and the lowest rates, so our site provides a guide to the task of picking out a broker.

More exciting than this, though, is the way the Internet has instantaneously released company information to all investors. No longer is it the preserve of the privileged institutional investors in the city and elsewhere. Now it is available to all of us through a number of sites, not least the company websites themselves. Most of the broker sites will carry RNS, the official regulatory news service. There are also the news wire services, namely

- **www.reuters.com**;
- **www.bloomberg.co.uk**;
- **www.bbc.co.uk**, the dear old BBC site, although its business news service is still pretty diabolical.

It's important to bear in mind that just because the news flow is more rapid these days it does not follow that investors need to deal more frequently. Results are just a snapshot of the company's performance at a point in time. Dealing on the back of results without full analysis of all the data can sometimes lead to hasty, and possibly mistaken, investment decisions. More free information is available at

- **www.financial-freebies.com**, which provides free copies of magazines and bulletins.

The main source of information on a company is the report and accounts.

- The Motley Fool, at **www.fool.co.uk**, allows you to order company reports and accounts online. They are then delivered by post.
- **www.carol.co.uk** allows you to read the reports online if you can't wait for snail-mail to deliver them.

Of course all FTSE 100 companies will have a website and will have a copy of their annual report online. Not every single company has its own website yet (although that will occur) and moving down the list of companies by size, there is less chance of finding the annual report online. Some companies do have superb websites, and I would spotlight Severn Trent Plc as a particularly good one. In fact it's so good that it won an award for Best Annual Report on the Internet in 1998 and 1997, and was commended in 1999. This site sets an excellent example for others. It includes graphs of the share price, analysts' presentations, a summary of earnings forecasts and recommendations from the analysts.

Now for a list of other sites that we're sure you'll find useful.

- **www.barbican.co.uk**. Although we don't much like unit trusts in general, this will give you heaps of data on them if you have one.
- **www.dismalscience.com** gives more detailed comment on economic issues, and is a site with a rare display of humility from economists.
- **www.lombardstreet.co.uk** gives further com-

mentary on economics.

- **www.londonstockexchange.co.uk** is the stock exchange website, and gives general information on the stock market.
- **www.bankofengland.co.uk** and
- **www.hm-treasury.gov.uk** give you information straight from the horse's mouth if you want to know how well (or how badly) the UK economy is doing; both are a mine of useful and interesting information.
- **www.ons.org.uk**, the Office of National Statistics, offers more data than you can poke a stick at.

If you find yourself getting confused by all the terminology, take a look at

- **www.fool.co.uk/glossary**, the glossary on our website;
- **www.plainenglish.co.uk/finance**; or
- **www.investorwords.com**.

And if you get tied up in all the technical jargon of some of these technology companies, then a good place to go for help is

- **www.whatis.com**, which explains the most arcane pieces of technical gobbledegook.

The Internet and technology companies also seem to generate acronyms by the yard. If you want to find out what they stand for have a look at

- **www.ucc.ie/info/net/acronyms/acro.html** or
- **www.acronymfinder.com**.

A continual scare story put out by the conventional media is the myth that the Internet, and discussion boards in particular, are populated by people trying to push or hype shares up so that other investors buy them at inflated prices. This process, often called ramping, is generally so transparent that it is obvious to all exactly what is going on. Discussion boards operate in much the same ways as queues. Everyone knows what the form is and if someone does try to push in they get short shrift from the others. Discussion boards become a similar mini-community and anyone trying to upset the order of play is obvious to all. On the Motley Fool site, posters to discussion boards are awarded points for the number of times they post messages and receive recommendations from other users for producing quality material. In addition, there is a mechanism by which users can alert Motley Fool staff to people who seem to be transgressing the rules of engagement. With these safeguards it is fairly easy to assess the quality of discussion underway, and once you get involved, the depth of information offered is astonishing.

Stay healthy

Interactive healthcare is still in its infancy, but it does have enormous possibilities. So far it is limited to the online NHS service that you can find at

- **www.nhsdirect.nhs.uk**.

Hypochondriacs should keep well away from this site, as they are sure to find something wrong with them, but for others the guide to ailments can be a very easy way of identifying ones that might be easily cured. If not, then it gives the phone number so that you can ring up and talk to a specially trained nurse. In years to come it is planned that NHS Direct, whether the online or telephone version, will become the first port of call for out-of-hours contact with your GP.

Conclusion

The invention of writing, the printing press, the telegraph, radio and television have all been powerful forces for change. But the Internet, which combines elements of all these media, is surely the most powerful of all. And there can be few better uses for it than helping us enrich ourselves and our lives so that we can enjoy a more comfortable retirement.

Chapter 10
The Fool's Guide to Wills

Here lies a poor woman who always was tired,
For she lived in a place where help wasn't hired.
Her last words on earth were, Dear Friend I am going
Where washing ain't done nor sweeping nor sewing
And everything there is exact to my wishes,
For there they don't eat and there's no washing of dishes...
Don't mourn me now, don't mourn me for never,
For I'm going to do nothing for ever and ever.
Epitaph in Bushey Churchyard, quoted in the
Spectator (1922)

It costs a lot of money to die comfortably.
Samuel Butler

This chapter deals with what happens when you shuffle off, snuff it, become deceased, exit, die. Most of us don't like to think about it, but it is going to happen. Everyone is going to be affected by illness and/or death at some stage, both their own and probably someone else's, too. It makes sense to plan for these eventualities and you can do it Foolishly without it costing you the earth, thus giving you peace of mind and the knowledge that your affairs are in tip-top order, whatever circumstances might arise. This chapter is largely adapted from a mini-series that runs on the Motley Fool site, written by Mark Goodson, one of the Motley Fool's freelance writers, who is a registered Trust and Estate Practitioner.

Trying to cover such a massive subject in just one chapter is a hard task, but it will give you the basics and equip you with the questions you need to ask, which is more than half the battle. You need to be aware of all the possible problems, solutions and outcomes, and then make up your own mind as to which course of action to take. But then that goes for pretty much everything we deal with at the Motley Fool.

The topics to be covered are:
1) Inheritance Tax: how it can be avoided
2) Wills and Trusts
3) Probate
4) Clearing up an inheritance tax mess
5) Other useful legal stuff

What we must stress, here and now, is that each person's objectives and circumstances are different. This means that it is impossible for any one person to read this chapter and then feel they have been equipped with all the knowledge they need to go and make watertight plans for their future. You should obtain a professional opinion wherever appropriate and be prepared to pay for that opinion. Contrary to popular belief, lawyers do not try to rip you off at every opportunity. They cannot survive on free 30-minute interviews, even though this is an extremely popular marketing tool. If you ask them to act, then it will cost you, so be prepared.

Also, make sure that the lawyer you consult has the necessary expertise in the field you require. The best conveyancer may make the worst litigator, and someone who got a fantastic result for your friend's personal injury claim might not have the first clue as to how to deal with your divorce. This is particularly relevant when dealing with the affairs of the elderly or the deceased, which is seen as very much the poor relation in legal offices; in fact, the work is generally passed on to inexperienced staff. So, if you decide you need to take legal advice, we would urge you to make sure the lawyer you consult is a member of STEP (The Society of Trust and Estate Practitioners). This is a self-regulatory worldwide society aiming to encompass the finest practitioners in this particular field. Members are entitled to use the initials TEP after their name, and this means that their expertise has been proven. A list of members can be obtained from STEP at their website (**www.step.org**) or from their offices at PO Box 13272, 110 Jermyn Street, London, SW1Y 6ZH, UK, telephone 020 7839 3886.

Here's an example from Mark's experience of how someone thought they could save a few bob by not taking professional advice:

I currently act for a lady whose sister died last year. Two years or so prior to her death, the deceased had some marital problems and she wanted to leave her estate to my client rather than to her husband. She did not want to make a home-made will, but also was unwilling to pay a professional. So, rather than see a lawyer, a friend of hers who worked for a firm of solicitors said that 'she would get a will done for her', which was prepared and intended to cover the marital problems, but the lady subsequently died without getting divorced.

There was, on the face of it, nothing wrong with the will; it gave her share of the property to my client (subject to a life interest for her husband) together with everything left after any expenses and legacies had been paid (the residue).

The problem is that her 'friend' was not sufficiently knowledgeable to know that joint property passes by survivorship, not by will. As the house was still in joint names with the husband when my client's sister died, he is now the proud owner of the property simply because he survived her. My client gets only the residue, which actually amounts to less than the debts and funeral expenses. So, in reality, all she will get is a bill. She could take court action, but this will be long-winded, expensive and not guaranteed to succeed.

This situation could have been avoided if the deceased had been prepared to pay the modest – and I mean modest – fee to have a professional will made.

Inheritance Tax: How it can be avoided

'The only certainties in life,' said Benjamin Franklin, famously, 'are death and taxes.' Ironic, then, that with Inheritance Tax (IHT) you get clobbered by both at the same time.

Well, it doesn't clobber everyone. The current IHT regime is quite lenient when compared to previous methods of calculating 'Death Duties', or 'Capital Transfer Tax', or whatever name it was known by. The top bracket was once 98 per cent tax. Seriously. No wonder there were once so many tax exiles.

So what is IHT? Well, it's a tax that is paid on your estate after your death at a flat rate of 40 per cent, subject to a few allowances and exemptions. Everyone, for instance, has a personal threshold (currently £234,000), which they are allowed to pass on prior to any tax being due. This threshold is very often referred to as the 'nil-rate band', because everything within it is taxable at a nil rate, i.e. zero. Over and above the threshold, tax is payable at 40 per cent. So, to use a simple example, Mrs Bloggs has an estate of £300,000. The threshold is deducted, leaving £66,000, and IHT is due at a rate of 40 per cent of that, leaving tax due of £26,400.

This is a very simple example. Certain beneficiaries are exempt from paying tax, for example the surviving spouse and charities. So, if Mrs Bloggs left a husband, and he inherited her entire estate, then the tax payable would be nil, because there is no tax due on inter-spouse transfers, regardless of the amount. Similarly, if Mrs Bloggs left the £66,000 (the amount in excess of the personal threshold) to charity in her will, then there would also be no tax payable because bequests to charities are exempt from tax.

But hold on a minute. Let's go back to Mr Bloggs. Let's say that he has £300,000 in his own name as well. His wife dies and, for the sake of argument, he inherits her entire estate of £300,000, and pays no IHT due to the spouse exemption. His estate, however, is now worth £600,000. When he dies, only his personal threshold will be deducted (we'll assume it stays at £234,000) leaving a net estate of £366,000. This whole amount is now taxable at 40 per cent, meaning a whopping tax bill of £146,400!

So what can be done to mitigate, or even avoid, the IHT due?

Well, in the case of Mr and Mrs Bloggs, they could have tax-efficient wills prepared, meaning that at least they each utilize their own personal threshold. This essentially means that the first of them to die leaves an amount equal to the nil-rate band (currently £234,000) to their children. Thus, on the death of the second, the estate will only be £366,000. Again the nil-rate band passes without tax, leaving just £132,000 to be taxed and a tax bill of only £53,000. So, this fairly simple task alone would save over £90,000 in IHT for the Bloggs' children.

They could also give money away to their children before death. If they live seven years after making the gift, then it would be completely free of IHT. Even before the seven years are up, the amount of IHT payable starts to reduce. But they would have to give it away completely; if they made a gift but reserved the right to use the money later if they needed it, then that would be a 'Gift with Reservation' and the Capital Taxes Office (CTO) would bring it into account.

There are various 'schemes' being promoted by some firms that rely on using the matrimonial home in tax planning. They can work in certain circumstances, but there is a feeling that the CTO are waiting to pounce on cases such as this, so it is generally considered best to avoid using the home if at all possible when planning for IHT.

Insurance companies are keen to sell IHT policies, i.e. those that pay out lump sums, to assist with any IHT burden. The premiums are generally very expensive though, and of course there are all those commissions to pay. Not very Foolish. Far better to put that amount to one side in a separate account, or make a gift of it to someone. There is an annual gift exemption of £3,000 to any one person as well as £250 to any number of people per year, and over the course of time, that amount of money can be removed from someone's taxable estate without the need to comply with the 'seven-year rule'.

The above are just some ways of mitigating IHT, and there are many others. But can you ever actually avoid it?

Well, yes, as long as you only want your family or friends to inherit the amount equivalent to the 'nil-rate' band. Anything over and above that must be given to charity. Here's an illustration of how two of Mark's wealthy clients did just that:

> *An elderly couple who had been life-long companions were unmarried. They found that the value of their assets and investments made them multi-millionaires. However, because they were only co-habitees, the spouse exemption for IHT would not apply if one of them were to die. So, on my advice, they got married and made simple wills giving everything to each other in the first instance and then to various charities (there are no children or other family). This guarantees that no IHT will be payable at all, and this was exactly what they wanted to achieve.*
>
> *I understand that they have now sent a schedule of their assets together with a copy of the wills to the Chancellor Gordon Brown, with a postcard that says 'HARD LUCK MATE!'*
>
> *Lovely.*

Wills and Trusts

Someone once said that there is nothing worse than dying without a will (intestate). Well, that's wrong. Dying with a will that was made 15 years ago and that has not been reviewed is much, much worse.

This is the problem, you see: wills don't go out of

date. Once made, they just sit there waiting for you to die, unless you revoke them by destroying them, making a new one or getting married.

So do you need to make a will? Well, do you? Are you one of those that think everything would go to your spouse? (It might, but only if your total estate is less than £200,000 and you have no children – £125,000 if there are children – or it is all held as joint property).

Or do you think that you don't own anything? (Really? No car, jewellery, house, life insurance, death in service benefit...?)

Or perhaps you are married with kids, mortgaged up to the hilt, and really have very few assets that could be disposed of by a will. (Right, what about your kids? Who would look after them if you and your spouse were both killed in an accident? You can and, if necessary, should appoint guardians in a will.)

Incidentally, certain conditions might allow you to get what used to be known as Legal Aid for the preparation of a will (for instance, if you are a single parent who wishes to appoint a guardian).

Anyway, here's a pretty simple guideline about when you need to make a will: if you have something to leave, then make one. It is the only way of guaranteeing that your property goes where you want it to go. And please, please, PLEASE don't go and get one of those pre-printed jobbies from a stationer for £3.50 just to save a few quid. It is a false economy to try and skimp on costs. Professional wills can cost as little as £50–£70 for a single and £95–£150 for husband and wife mirror wills, depending on where you go. The costs involved in sorting out badly worded or incorrect home-made wills after your death could run into four figures or more. This is a perfect example of when being Foolish means NOT doing it yourself.

Since we do think you should use a professional for your will, we won't go into detail about how to make one, but will highlight a few possible loopholes and problems you should consider.

1) Appointing executors. These are the people who have to sort everything out on your demise. There is a common misconception that you cannot be an executor and a beneficiary. Of course you can! This is the most common type of will in the world ('I give my entire estate to my wife and appoint her sole executor'). However, you cannot be a beneficiary (or the spouse of a beneficiary) and a witness to the will. This would invalidate the gift, but not the will. Appointing independent professionals is a good idea if you think there may be problems. Otherwise close family (preferably those of your own age or younger, for obvious reasons) will be fine. Be careful about appointing friends, too – this often seems to run into problems.

2) Making gifts. Please bear in mind that you are making the will now, but you may well live for many, many years. Therefore, try not to be woolly. Don't, for instance, give all the money in a certain account to a beneficiary. When you die, the account may not exist, or may have far less or far more in it than you intend the beneficiary to receive. Far better to leave a round amount or a percentage.

3) At what age do you want your children or grandchil-

dren to receive their legacy? If no age is specified, the law says they can give a valid receipt at 18, but not beforehand. But would you want your kids to inherit a large sum of money at 18? Would they be mature enough to handle it? How long do you think it would last?

4) Do you want to place assets in trust? Aaah, trusts. These can be highly complex beasts. There are Discretionary Trusts, Life Interest Trusts, Will Trusts, Bare Trusts, Accumulation and Maintenance Trusts, Secret Trusts... such a subject is far too vast for us to attempt to do justice to here. However, for a trust to be effective, it has to have three qualities, known as the 'three certainties'. It must a) have a subject, b) be clear that it is a trust, and c) be possible to list the beneficiaries exactly. A simple trust in a will may be to give a freehold property (the subject) to any grand-children (the beneficiaries), that survive the deceased and who also attain the age of 25, subject to the chil-dren of the deceased having the use and benefit of the house for their lifetime (this is the bit that creates the trust). Phew.

A nil-rate band Discretionary Trust in a will for married couples is pretty tax-efficient, but the trust wording runs to several pages and is very complex. Different trusts have different purposes and different tax advantages, so if you think a trust may help you then you *must* take professional advice.

Probate: some questions and answers

Er, what's probate?

Here is a phrase that occurs with incredible regularity: 'I want to make a will because I don't want my children to have to go to probate.' This is probably the most common misconception that people have when deciding to make a will. It's wrong.

Right, let's start with the basics. The word *probate* is derived from the Latin word meaning 'prove it', and a Grant of Probate is what has to be obtained when a will is proved, i.e. submitted to the court after someone has died.

If someone dies without making a will, however, then they are said to have died *intestate*. In this instance, the grant from the court is called 'Letters of Administration'. There are other types of special grant, but generally the court order enabling the personal representatives to deal with an estate is called the 'Grant of Representation'. However, most people refer to the grant as a Grant of Probate because it rolls off the tongue slightly more easily. The process of obtaining this grant is referred to as 'probate'.

Who are the personal representatives?

If there is a will, the personal representative is the executor. If there is no will (known as an intestacy) then the personal representative is generally the next of kin. There is a statutory order that stipulates exactly who is entitled to act in this capacity. In certain circumstances, a residuary beneficiary or a creditor can also apply for a Grant of Probate.

To make matters a whole lot more fun, sometimes there can be what is called a partial intestacy. This occurs when a will does not dispose of all of the assets of the deceased because it has been badly worded. In cases like this, all property not referred to in the will is distributed according to the law of intestacy, which very broadly speaking means that the next of kin gets it (depending on how much it is and whether the next of kin is the surviving spouse or not). This is where winding up an estate can take many years and cost an absolute fortune. Imagine if your next of kin were your cousins (or their children, if the cousins had predeceased you). Do you know how to contact them? And if you have died, how are your executors going to find them? This is one of the most common problems of the home-made will. A person doesn't know exactly how to word it, makes a hash of it, and the end result is that the administration of his estate takes several years and costs many thousands of pounds because he wanted to save himself £50. Doesn't make sense to me.

So why does it take so long to wind up someone's estate?

What has to be understood is that when someone dies, a line has to be drawn under their affairs for good. Before the estate can be wound up, it is essential that all assets are claimed and all liabilities are discharged. With regard to liabilities, these may not just be what was owed at the time of death; there may also be claims against the estate. In law, a claim can be made in respect of a debt or inheritance claim for up to six months *after the date of the Grant of Probate!* Not the date of death, the date of the grant. So it will typically take two to three months to collect the necessary information in order to apply for the grant. Once the relevant affidavits are sworn and the papers lodged with the court, the grant can take up to four weeks to be issued. *Then* the six-month clock starts running. See? We're up to nine or ten months already! This is why an executor has one year from the date of death before anyone can say that he is 'dragging his feet', so to speak. So if you are a beneficiary under a will, don't think it is taking a long time just because three months have passed. Have patience.

Will making a will give my executors immediate access to my money when I die?

No. Here we have a Catch-22 situation. First you have to ascertain the size of the estate, so that the probate papers can be prepared. Then a grant can be applied for, but only after any Inheritance Tax has been paid. But you can't get access to the funds without obtaining a grant.

So I can't get the grant until I've paid the tax?

Correct.

But I can't pay the tax until I get the money, and I can't get the money until I get the grant!

Correct again.

But I can't get the grant until I've paid the tax!

Going around in circles now, aren't we? There are ways

around it and it's not all that difficult, but again it's wise to employ professionals in complicated cases because they know the correct procedures, which can save a lot of stress and heartache for the bereaved relatives.

Clearing up an IHT mess

After reading the previous parts of this chapter you could possibly be forgiven for thinking that it would be an absolute nightmare if someone close to you were to die having made no planning whatsoever in their lifetime. Well, it can be, but sometimes there are things you can do.

We have already covered, briefly, what happens if someone dies without a will, and further on we talk about what happens if someone has no Power of Attorney; but current legislation allows people to make some retrospective tax planning. Here is a typical example of how it might work.

Let's say that your parents are both in their eighties and have not made wills. Their combined estates add up to £500,000. Suddenly your father dies. The house, we will assume, is in joint names and is worth £200,000, and there are bank accounts and other investments also in joint names (a few privatization shares perhaps). There is nothing to do on his death as everything passes by survivorship (remember our earlier section), and your mother therefore inherits the lot. Distribution under the Law of Intestacy does not come into effect because there is no estate to administer.

However, when she dies, assuming she still has £500,000, then there will be an Inheritance Tax bill of over £106,000. Ouch!

Can anything be done about this? Of course. TA-TA-TA-DA! TA-TA-TA-TA-TA-TA-DA! ENTER THE CAVALRY!

Well, enter the 'Deed of Variation', anyway. This is a perfectly legal instrument that can be used to mitigate or avoid IHT provided that it is effected within two years of the date of death. Let's explain how it works.

We have already established that, in our example, your mother is in her eighties and is worth £500,000. The house is worth £200,000, with the rest in cash or liquid investments. Does an eighty-something-year-old woman really need £300,000 cash plus her pension? Quite possibly not.

If she was willing, she could enter into a Deed of Variation, which could give a sum equivalent to the nil-rate band (currently £234,000) to the children, and it would be deemed to come straight from the estate of their late father. This means that when she dies, her estate will only be worth £266,000. After deduction of the personal threshold of £234,000, the taxable estate is only £32,000, which equates to a liability of only £12,800 at 40 per cent. This represents a saving of over £90,000, and all for the modest cost of probably only a few hundred quid. Pretty Foolish.

Now, there are some conditions and downsides to this:

1) The deed must be effected within two years of the date of death;

2) The variation must be made by the person or persons who will be disadvantaged by it, and if they don't agree then it cannot be effected;

3) It won't work if the principal asset is the matrimonial home and the surviving spouse is resident there alone; and

4) The government may abolish or amend this legislation at any time.

So, all in all, it probably is best to make proper lifetime planning rather than leave it to chance. A Deed of Variation is a rescue measure that may or may not be effective, depending on the particular circumstances.

Other useful legal stuff

Powers of Attorney

We've covered wills pretty thoroughly, but they only come into effect when you die. So what if you have a stroke or a bad accident, which leaves you physically and/or mentally incapable of managing your affairs? In that case, what you need to have is a Power of Attorney. This is a document that appoints a person or persons to act on your behalf if you are unable to do so yourself. There are currently two types, general and enduring.

A general Power of Attorney applies where someone is physically incapable of managing their affairs. It can give general authority to the attorney or it can be very specific. For instance, someone could be appointed to act as an attorney in the signing of a contract if the donor is out of the country. No power is taken away from the donor but, quite simply, power is given to a third party or parties. More than one person can be appointed to act and they can act independently of each other (joint and several) or both together (joint).

An enduring Power, however, is far more powerful, because it is intended to continue if the donor becomes mentally incapable. This confers tremendous responsibility on the attorney, who has a duty to register the Power with the Court of Protection if the donor has become, or is becoming, mentally incapable. The registration process is onerous and costs money, but this pales into insignificance compared to the process of appointing a receiver for a patient who is mentally incapable and who has NOT got an enduring Power of Attorney. This takes many months, costs a fortune and the receiver then has to account to the Court of Protection annually for all the income and expenditure of the patient. To rub salt into the wound, the court also takes a slice of the annual income for the privilege of overseeing the accounts.

An enduring Power of Attorney has been likened to an insurance policy. Absolutely useless unless it is required, but if you haven't got one when you need it then it's too late.

Full details of the process, and a very helpful little booklet explaining everything in much more detail is available from:

Enduring Power of Attorney Team
Public Trust Office
Protection Division
Stewart House
24 Kingsway
London
WC2B 6JX
EPA Helpline 020 7664 7327

Notices of Severance

These are simple documents that are used to sever the joint tenancy of a property. Most joint property is held as beneficial joint tenancies, which means that in the event of the death of one of the owners then the other takes the property by survivorship, as we dealt with earlier. Such property does not form part of a person's estate and does not get dealt with according to the terms of a will.

However, a Notice of Severance will 'sever the joint tenancy' so that each party will own, usually, 50 per cent of the property, although the percentages can be uneven, for instance 70/30. This means that their share of the property CAN be dealt with by a will and it is a useful planning tool which might mitigate Inheritance Tax or protect assets.

Funeral plans

It's Foolish to plan your funeral, but it's not so Foolish to pay for it now – that's just like an expensive life assurance policy.

Think carefully about your last requests, though. You don't want to place a burden on those you leave behind. My father-in-law died unexpectedly but, being a retired bank manager, he had made a will and all his affairs were in order. However, his whole life had been devoted to steam trains – watching and photographing them. His final requests to do with his hobby gave his widow more trouble than anything else. Apart from having to ring sundry rail museums to 'donate' (which really meant dump) stacks of photographs, she had the slight problem of his ashes to deal with. Philip had lived most of his life near the east coast main line, not far from Essendine where the Mallard had made its famous record-breaking run. He wanted his ashes to join the famous cinders on British Rail's permanent way. But how was Muriel, his widow, going to achieve that? Would she, a granny, have to tiptoe on to the rails risking the wrath of a Railtrack inspector for trespassing, not to mention the potential mortal effect of getting in the way of a Virgin Express trying to run on time? Perhaps she should buy a ticket on the self-same train and spread the ashes from that? Again problems presented themselves. If she opened the window, might the draught not blow the ashes back into the carriage and all over her fellow passengers? That would never do. Anyway she hates draughts.

What if the train was air-conditioned? Then no windows would open and the posthumous defenestrating of her loved one would be impossible. The only other means of depositing matter on the track, in loo of an alternative, could not be considered. In the end this practical girl-guiding matron hit on a very pragmatic solution. On her way back from Tescos one day she stopped the car on the Essendine bridge and dumped the contents of the urn over the parapet. Problem solved, but it did cause her a lot of anguish.

Protecting assets from the local authority

'Why would I want to do that?' you say. Well, since Care in the Community was introduced, people going into residential or nursing care have basically lost their assets (and sometimes even been made bankrupt) in order to pay for it. Present rules allow you to keep £16,000. The cost of care can be £20,000 per year and it doesn't take long to whittle away someone's estate at that rate.

You might, however, be able to pass on some assets to others, such as your children, causing the local authority to pay for your care if that becomes necessary. Beware, though: this is *provided* that there is not already any reason why you should feel that you might need nursing care. If a patient has been diagnosed as having Alzheimer's, then this is what is known as regressive; i.e. it does not get better, only worse. So, even if the disease is in its infancy, the chances are that an Alzheimer's sufferer will need permanent nursing care at some point. Therefore, once diagnosed with any regressive disease, if the patient disposes of their assets in order that the local authority will have to pick up the tab for their care, they will be treated as having made a 'deprivation', and the family of the patient (or the recipients of the assets) will be pursued. And they do it, believe me.

The cost of care can be funded through a mixture of benefits and income. A homeowner in the south-east who has a state pension, Attendance Allowance, perhaps an occupational pension and approximately £70,000 in liquid assets can probably fund residential care and still protect their estate.

Let's look at the case of a married elderly couple, both in good health and who are cash poor, property rich. First of all, they should not worry about losing their home if one should need care. The home is disregarded by the local authority if another relative over 60 is living in it. As you can keep £16,000 of your own money, this effectively means that a couple have to have in excess of £32,000 between them before they are required to pick up the tab for their care. They may have to make a small contribution depending on the home they own, but this should be easily affordable.

But what happens in the event of one dying and the other needing care? To cover that eventuality, it is worth severing their joint tenancy, or taking whatever other measures are necessary to ensure that they hold it as tenants in common in equal shares. Then, in a will, they should give each respective half of the property to their children, or whomever they wish. This in itself poses other potential problems, i.e. possible claims by children's partners in the event of divorce, but generally the survivor has right of occupation and so cannot be slung out.

Going through the above steps means that, after the first death, half the property is now held by the children, and half by the survivor.

Here's an example:

Mr and Mrs Bloggs own their house, worth £70,000, jointly. They have little or no savings. Mrs Bloggs dies, and the house passes by survivorship to Mr Bloggs.

Mr Bloggs then needs care. He will be assessed, and, assuming the property stays at the same value, his house will be charged with up to £54,000 of care. If the house stays empty, the care bill will take approximately three years to reach that level. If the house is sold, then the money can be invested and it will last a bit longer.

However, if Mr and Mrs B had made wills in accordance with the above, then on Mrs B's death half the property would have passed to the kids immediately. This means that the local authority could only charge half the property LESS the £16,000 allowance, i.e. only £19,000 of care. This would protect the bulk of the house value for the children.

There are other ways of losing assets without creating

a deprivation. For instance, if Mr B had the house and £25,000 in cash he did not rely on, the purchase of personal chattels (including fine art or antiques) would not be considered a deprivation. So a Patek Phillipe watch might fit the bill. Also, if any of the cash held is as a result of a personal injury claim, or some form of compensation, then that too is disregarded.

Finally, if Mr B needed care, and he had a relative over 60 who was living in his house, then the value of the property would still be disregarded and (depending on his other assets) the local authority would foot the care bill.

As you can see, it is a complicated area and we can only really go into general situations here.

The Annual Gift Exemption and tax-free investments

These are little-used planning aids that can help to significantly reduce an estate for IHT purposes. There is an annual gift exemption of £3,000 that can be given free of any IHT to any one person. There is also an exemption that applies to annual amounts of £250 to any number of people. There are special exemptions for gifts to children in the year they marry, as well as other special exemptions too. Professional advice is required, but it doesn't take a genius to work out that if you gift just £3,000 per year for 20 years to your family, then that's £60,000 less in your estate at the time of your death – a tax saving of £24,000.

Conclusion

Wills and estate planning is a crucial issue to most people in retirement, but it is also one of the most difficult areas to address. Not only are the rules complex, but the issues can be highly emotive. The best approach is to think carefully about what it is that you want to achieve and then seek professional advice. If you do it the other way around, you could end up paying for something that doesn't solve your problems.

Afterword

That last chapter was a fitting way to end, for end it must eventually, for all of us. We sincerely hope this book will help you plan for a secure retirement so that the time leading up to that ending is as happy and prosperous as possible.

If it was necessary to extract just one lesson from these pages, a lesson you'll take away with you and keep close long after the book itself is mouldering on the rack in the Oxfam shop, it's this: start early. Now, that might sound dispiriting if you're reading this and are anywhere North of 25 years old, but it shouldn't, because 'Start early' really translates as 'However young you are, however old you are, however late you think you've left it, doing something NOW is a lot better than doing it later.' That doesn't mean you should rush precipitately into action, but it does mean you should start an active planning process NOW, this minute, which will lead, within a reasonable timeframe, into action.

So, that's it. There are no great memory or learning feats involved in planning for your retirement. There are no great intellectual requirements. Nor does it take a tremendous amount of time. The basic facts you need to know and understand are simple and available in many places – in this book and our other books, on the Web, in newspapers and magazines – and can therefore be accessed at will. Hopefully, this book will have given you some insights in and of itself, and will have pointed you in the direction of further sources of assistance. All you need to keep repeating to yourself, all you need to remember, as you put it down and embark upon the process of retirement planning are those two short words: 'Start early!'

And with that, it remains only to wish you a very happy and a very Foolish retirement.